Discovery Tool Cookbook:
Recipes for Successful Lesson Plans

edited by Nancy Fawley and Nikki Krysak

Association of College and Research Libraries
A division of the American Library Association

Chicago • 2016

The paper used in this publication meets the minimum requirements of American National Standard for Information Sciences-Permanence of Paper for Printed Library Materials, ANSI Z39.48-1992. ∞

The ACRL Cookbook series was conceived of and designed by Ryan Sittler and Doug Cook.
Other books in this series:

The Library Instruction Cookbook by Ryan L. Sittler and Douglas Cook
The Embedded Librarian's Cookbook edited by Kaijsa Calkins and Cassandra Kvenild

Library of Congress Cataloging-in-Publication Data

Names: Fawley, Nancy, editor. | Krysak, Nikki, editor
Title: Discovery tool cookbook : recipes for successful lesson plans / edited
    by Nancy Fawley and Nikki Krysak.
Description: Chicago : Association of College and Research Libraries, a
    division of the American Library Association, 2016.
Identifiers: LCCN 2016010123 | ISBN 9780838988916 (pbk. : alk. paper)
Subjects: LCSH: Library orientation for college students. | Online
    bibliographic searching--Study and teaching (Higher) | Electronic
    information resource searching--Study and teaching (Higher) | Internet
    searching--Study and teaching (Higher) | Research--Methodology--Study and
    teaching (Higher)
Classification: LCC Z711.25.C65 D57 2016 | DDC 025.5/677--dc23 LC record available at http://lccn.loc.
gov/2016010123

Printed in the United States of America.

20 19 17 17 16   5 4 3 2 1

TABLE OF CONTENTS

Table of Contents

Acknowledgements

Like many instruction librarians, we struggle with the limitations of a one-shot library session. There is never enough time to address the basic skills necessary to successfully search a database, *and* delve into the conceptual skills that contribute to student success and lifelong learning. Instead we found ourselves doing the usual dog and pony show of "click here, click there" to assist students in finding the resources needed for their research assignment.

The widespread implementation of discovery tools opened up new possibilities for instruction for us. We no longer had to dedicate valuable class time to teach basic search skills. While the tools are intuitive to use, we soon found that the interface could also compound existing challenges to locating well-rounded, accurate information about certain topics, creating many opportunities for teachable moments. Designed for a Google generation with proprietary algorithms that determine which research databases are included, discovery tools as the "new library catalog" opened up a conversation that naturally drifted toward the key themes of the ACRL *Framework for Information Literacy for Higher Education*.

Our research and webinars that we have conducted to date focused on librarian attitudes about discovery tools, but we soon found that what people really needed were hands-on lesson plans that could be adapted to meet individual classroom settings. This book is the natural result of what needed to follow. Each recipe aligns itself with at least one ACRL *Frame* and includes special areas of focus within the Knowledge Practices and Dispositions associated with those frames. These correspond with student learning outcomes for each lesson.

The editing process began as we both embarked on new jobs and adventures. We would like to thank our new colleagues at our respective institutions who have inspired us with their knowledge and creativity. A nod is also due to Ryan L. Sittler and Douglas Cook for the original cookbook idea and kicking off what is now a series of themed lesson plans masquerading as intercontinental recipes. A special thank you goes out to Kathryn Deiss for believing in the value of our idea and to Dawn Mueller for her master edits. We also extend our thanks to each author who contributed their ideas to this book. We wouldn't have a book without your kitchen experimentation!

Thanks to our families for their encouragement and patience during the detailed and long-winded editing process. Last but not least, Nikki and Nancy recognize their immense gratitude for each other, two Pisceans who managed to avoid going over the waterfall.

HOW TO CONTACT US:
Nancy Fawley
Director, Information & Instruction Services, University of Vermont
nfawley@uvm.edu

Nikki Krysak
Library Director, St. Johnsbury Academy
nikki.krysak@gmail.com

INTRODUCTION

How to Use This Book

This cookbook is separated into six chapters, each representing a different celebratory aspect of the menu-design process:

- **Starters:** Warm up activities, meta-cognitive moments to transition to the main "meal"
- **The Larder:** Short activities to have on hand that can be used when needed. These can be added in or used as substitutions in other lesson plans.
- **Tapas:** Shared (group) activities
- **Meal Plans:** Full lesson plans for single or multiple instruction sessions
- **Regional Fare:** Lesson plans for international students, faculty, and K–12
- **Room Service:** Flipping the classroom: lesson plans that incorporate pre-class work

Each lesson featured in this book was chosen for its adaptability to be custom-suited to your own classroom learning outcomes. Some are particularly good to acquaint high school students with the research-ready path demanded in first-year university settings. Others assume a level of research expertise ideal to graduate students. Know your audience and use your judgement to adapt as required.

True to the core of past *Cookbook* editions, each recipe is peppered with the following information to guide you through your own meal-planning:

Nutrition Information is a short introduction to each recipe that includes student learning outcomes.

Number Served represents the optimal class size.

Cooking Time indicates required prep time as well as time needed for actual lesson delivery. Plan ahead and make sure you have all ingredients ahead of time!

Dietary Guidelines feature at least one ACRL *Frame* with corresponding Knowledge Practices and Dispositions. These link back to student learning outcomes specified in *Nutrition Information*.

Ingredients & Equipment are essential to the success of each recipe. Substitutions are always encouraged depending on your own dining audience, but make sure you think ahead to consider the outcome of changing key ingredients.

Preparation gives you a step-by-step rundown of how to get your stuff chopped, boiling, and ready to serve. Follow the directions. Don't get lazy and skip steps, especially on your first try.

Cooking Method is the lesson plan, step-by-step. Feel free to improvise, add your own special sauce, and make the recipe your own!

Allergy Warnings are helpful tips from the authors based on their kitchen experiences.

Chef's Notes are the author's comments and anecdotes.

Clean Up (if included) gives suggestions and examples of assessment methods to close the loop.

Most recipes have additional information in the form of handouts, rubrics, or links to examples. Use these to enhance your own custom blend.

Remember, not all discovery tools come equipped with the same features. A good cook will improvise based on individual kitchen ingredients, dietary preferences, and who's coming over for dinner.

Bon Appétit!

1. STARTERS

warm up activities

Peer-Reviewed Journals as Geek-Out Message Boards:
Using Analogies to Describe Publication Types

Dr. Smita Avasthi, Lead Instruction Librarian, Santa Rosa Junior College, savasthi@santarosa.edu

NUTRITION INFORMATION

This recipe can be used to help students select sources when faced with a result list from the discovery tool. As the result list will include a wide range of publication types, this activity will help students make informed choices about which publication type to consult. It allows you to describe publication types to students by focusing on how the expertise level of the intended audience affects the content of a source.

Learning Outcomes
Students will be able to:
- Find information efficiently and effectively using a discovery tool.
- Select publications appropriate to their research topic.

NUMBER SERVED
20 to 40 students

COOKING TIME
Preparation time is minimal.
Lesson delivery: approximately 15 to 20 minutes

DIETARY GUIDELINES
Frame: Searching as Strategic Exploration

Knowledge Practices:
- Utilize divergent (e.g., brainstorming) and convergent (e.g., selecting the best source) thinking when searching.
- Match information needs and search strategies to appropriate search tools.

Dispositions:
- Exhibit mental flexibility and creativity.
- Realize that information sources vary greatly in content and format and have varying relevance and value, depending on the needs and nature of the search.

INGREDIENTS & EQUIPMENT
- Projector
- Instructor's computer
- Whiteboard (optional)
- It's useful to have access to student computer workstations for any activity planned after this starter, but the recipe itself doesn't call for them.

PREPARATION
- Prior to the class, identify a topic that you are passionate about and on which you have a high level of expertise (preferably something other than library science). The best results will reveal a passion or interest that may be unexpected or is related to popular culture.
- Start this lesson after familiarizing students with the results list of a discovery tool by conducting a basic search. Zero in on a set of results that includes a few different publication types in addition to a peer-reviewed journal. Point out that the discovery tool retrieves multiple types of publications.

COOKING METHOD
1. Engage the class in a discussion that may seem tangential. Begin by asking them to identify a passion or an interest. I describe this interest as "something you are slightly obsessed with, something that perhaps you think about a little too often. Maybe your friends have asked you not to talk about it quite so much." I also tell them that I will reveal my own interest once I hear a few of their passions.
2. After a few students volunteer, I reveal my obsession (usually, I refer to Harry Potter, Star Trek, and/or Game of Thrones). I then describe how I became interested in this topic and how my "obsession" with it led me to seek out other people with a similar degree of interest in the subject.
3. Then, I describe my experience of communicating with people who are also

very interested in the topic. I introduce the term "discourse community" when describing how we developed a shorthand method of communicating, including abbreviations and acronyms. I portray these conversations as if they are part of a "geek out message board" which would be confusing to anyone who was not in that discourse community.

4. At this point, I launch a 10-minute think-pair-share activity:
   » **Think:** I ask students to identify a topic on which they have a great deal of expertise and to think about how they discuss that topic when they talk to other experts. Then, I ask them to compare and contrast that conversation with the one they have when discussing that topic with someone who is not an expert yet.
   » **Pair:** Students then pair up and describe the differences they discovered when comparing and contrasting the varied audience.
   » **Share:** Ask students to share the differences that they noticed. Capture those points on a white board.

5. When I have a list of traits (i.e., "I use different vocabulary" or "I get right to the point" when talking to experts, vs. "I have to explain things" or "I don't use details but just outline the big picture" when talking to non-experts), I draw analogies between those traits and the qualities associated with a peer-reviewed journal in contrast to a reference entry.

6. Depending on the answers, I can draw straight parallels. For instance, "I use different vocabulary" is easily linked to the specialized language found in a peer-reviewed journal. However, you may find that you need to make the analogy work when students describe a feature of the conversation where the similarities are not as obvious.
   » For example, students may need help in seeing how "I get right to the point" may relate to the verbosity of a peer-reviewed journal, so I often refer to the scope of the article. I demonstrate that peer-reviewed articles have a narrow focus by reviewing titles. I explain that zeroing in on one small aspect of a large topic without providing an overview of the topic is how experts may "get right to the point." I then contrast that narrow focus with the "big picture" that you find in a reference article.

7. End with a five-minute overview of other common publication types while demonstrating the use of the "source type" limiter. Explain the value in consulting a range of publication types. Point out that the discovery tool allows them to select different publication types on the same topic by conducting a single search. Suggest a potential research plan, such as starting with a reference article before exploring books and journals to collect a range of sources. Explain that they can find an overview and highly detailed specific data by conducting one search and using the source limiter wisely.

ALLERGY WARNINGS

You may find that students are reluctant to share their passions or interests. Once a brave student volunteers, reward that student by appearing impressed and delighted by their interest. If a student brings up a passion you know nothing about, refer to that topic when describing a reference article. For instance, a student might say s/he's passionate about baseball. If so, I would refer to that topic when explaining that I'd want to consult a reference book if I were going to a baseball game. This helps to dispel notions that the "best" sources are peer-reviewed; use the variety of their interests to show that we all have varying levels of expertise and should choose source based upon what will help us learn about the topic.

CHEF'S NOTE

This activity is particularly useful if the main course allows students to conduct hands-on research so they can experiment with the limiter. However, it could work as a starter to another activity if the classroom is not equipped with computer workstations.

I have found that this activity may start slowly and it can require some quick thinking on your feet if the discussion doesn't go as intended, but students nearly always enjoy hearing about my passions and interests. It brings a "human" element to the one-shot and helps me make connections with students, which can often be difficult during a short encounter. I have found that they are more attentive and responsive once they see me as a person with interests. I have also found that students always remember the story I told them about my passions when they come by the reference desk. I believe this personal anecdote makes me more approachable and helps to make that crucial connection with students.

CLEAN UP

I have used a simple assessment tool at the end of the one-shot which includes multiple choice questions. Some of these questions are based upon their experience with the one-shot in general, and some questions are designed to check for their knowledge. I will include a question about when to use peer-reviewed journals, and I have found a very high percentage (usually between 85 to 100 percent) of students answer this question correctly.

ADDITIONAL RESOURCES

Here is an example of a multiple choice question that you can add to an assessment:

Peer-reviewed journals are most likely to be useful when I…
- A. am already familiar with my topic.
- B. need a short article that I can read quickly.
- C. am looking for an overview of my topic.
- D. need to find definitions of words or concepts related to my topic.

Sampling the Menu:
Exploring Search Results in Discovery Tools

Natalie Burclaff, Head of Information Literacy Initiatives, University of Baltimore, nburclaff@ubalt.edu

NUTRITION INFORMATION
This recipe gives students a chance to discuss search results as a group, and creates an appetite for exploring discovery tools.

Learning Outcomes
Students will be able to:
- Describe the different types of sources in a discovery tool search result list.
- Identify at least three related keywords to a given broad topic.
- Compare approaches to the same topic by different source types.

NUMBER SERVED
0 to 40 students, for a large group discussion

COOKING TIME
10 minutes, with minimal preparation.

DIETARY GUIDELINES
Frame: Searching as Strategic Exploration

Knowledge Practices:
- Understand how information systems are organized in order to access relevant information.
- Manage searching processes and results effectively.

Dispositions:
- Understand that first attempts at searching do not always produce adequate results.
- Realize that information sources vary greatly in content and format and have varying relevance and value, depending on the needs and nature of the search.

INGREDIENTS & EQUIPMENT
- Internet access for students
- Dry erase board

PREPARATION
- To prepare, select a recent topic in the news that is broad enough to be analyzed in multiple ways.
- Try searching the topic ahead of time to make sure the discovery tool brings up a variety of different sources on the first page.

COOKING METHOD
1. Using a recent news topic, have students brainstorm different perspectives or lenses people might use to talk about the topic. Keep track of the ideas on a whiteboard, smart board, or easel in the front of the classroom (Figure 1).

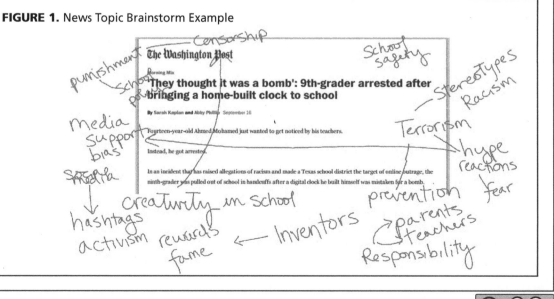

FIGURE 1. News Topic Brainstorm Example

2. Navigate the students to the discovery tool. Select a few broad keywords generated by the brainstorming activity and have everyone search using the same keyword(s) on the topic.

3. Give the students two minutes to browse the first page of results to identify what people are saying about the topic and which source types are used to discuss the topic.

4. After the two minutes, have select students share what they discovered in the first page of results. Point out when the subtopics or perspectives match what students previously brainstormed. Use this to talk about subject headings, and the importance of keywords.

5. Bring attention to the topics of news and magazine articles versus scholarly sources, and use that as a starting point for a conversation about difference between types of sources, and when they might be useful.

ALLERGY WARNINGS
Pick a topic that will be appetizing to the class, and that most students would be able to brainstorm around. For quiet classes, brainstorming prompts like how a specific profession might view the topic can help generate conversation; it also helps to have student write down ideas before sharing.

CHEF'S NOTE
This activity gives them a taste of what is in a discovery tool. Many times students as-sume that if a source is found through the library, it must be academic. They also see the different flavors of one particular topic, which is a great segue into having them brainstorm their own research interests.

CLEAN UP
The group discussion about the search results and brainstorm notes on the whiteboard act as a formative assessment. Additionally, students can write down their observations of the search results page and these can be collected and used as an assessable artifact. An optional assessment that can translate to a larger activity is to have students search their research topics, and identify a subtopic based on the search results. Have students find an additional source on that subtopic, and justify why that particular source is relevant and appropriate (in terms of type of source).

Hold *The Onion*, Please:
A Game Where Students Guess Which News Headlines Are Fake and Which Are Real

Amanda Gorrell, Public Services Librarian, Northwest Vista College, agorrell2@alamo.edu

NUTRITION INFORMATION

This recipe is a fun way to introduce students to searching for credible news articles through your library discovery tool vs. the internet. Students will compete in groups to guess which of three news headlines is from the infamous satire news site, *The Onion*.

Learning Outcomes

Students will be able to:

- Describe the inherent biases that can come with searching the internet in order to effectively evaluate information on their topic.
- Explain the differences between how information is selected and indexed in a library discovery tool vs. a search engine in order to choose the best search tool for their information needs.

NUMBER SERVED

10 to 28 students

COOKING TIME

Prep time: 20 minutes to create PowerPoint
Lesson Delivery: 20 minutes

DIETARY GUIDELINES

Frame: Searching as Strategic Exploration

Knowledge Practices:

- Utilize divergent (e.g., brainstorming) and convergent (e.g., selecting the best source) thinking when searching.
- Understand how information systems (i.e., collections of recorded information) are organized in order to access relevant information.

Disposition:

Realize that information sources vary greatly in content and format and have varying relevance and value, depending on the needs and nature of the search.

INGREDIENTS & EQUIPMENT

- Computers for students with internet access
- Instructor station
- Projector
- Numbered (1, 2 & 3) index cards.
- Candy or other prizes

PREPARATION

- Prepare four PowerPoint slides. Each slide should contain three news article headlines numbered 1, 2 and 3. Two headlines from a real news source and one from the satirical news site *The Onion*. You can also add a fun or humorous photo. Try to focus on the same topic for each group of headlines. For example, one slide could contain headlines that deal with the topic of gun control. Prepare numbered (1, 2 & 3) index cards to give to each group of students.

COOKING METHOD

1. Split students into small groups, giving each group a set of numbered cards.
2. Explain the rules: When you show a slide each group has 30 seconds to determine which of the three headlines is fake by holding up the corresponding numbered card. Award points to the group that answers correctly and give prizes to the group that has the most points at the end of the game.
3. After the game is over, start a discussion with your students about satirical news sites by asking if anyone has ever heard of *The Onion*. If no one has, explain that the purpose of satirical news sites is not to present real facts but to use satire (irony, sarcasm, ridicule) to comment on local and global events, politics, government and society in an attempt to show shortcomings. Other satirical news sites you can refer to during discussion include *The Daily Currant*, *World News Daily Report*, *The National Report* and *Call the Cops*.

4. Ask your students to pull up *The Onion* website and your library discovery tool. Have students compare the two pages and explain the differences by shouting out answers to you. What clues do students see that would indicate that one site is more credible than the other? *The Onion* has several red flags on their website that students should pick up on including fake headlines and fake weather reports.

5. Next ask the class to following along on their computers as you do a search on both *The Onion* and in the discovery tool for the same topic. Have students compare both search result lists and answer the following questions. Do the headlines look similar? Is there any way to refine the search to get better results? Do both tools provide bibliographic information? How does this help you evaluate the sources?

ALLERGY WARNINGS
Even in groups, students can be shy about answering. Sometimes they wait for another group to hold up a number and then choose the same one. Emphasize that this is a competition and there are prizes for the winning team. Additionally, some groups can move through the game very fast while others take a bit longer. Speed can vary by class and searching experience.

CHEF'S NOTE
Some students are very surprised to find out which headlines are real and which are fake. I have had entire classes that have never heard of *The Onion* or other fake news/satirical websites before. If you do have a class in which some students are familiar with *The Onion,* ask them to describe it to their fellow classmates and tell them why it is not a good resource to go to for information. I have even had instructors tell their classes stories about previous students citing *The Onion* in research assignments.

CLEAN UP
You can assess student learning outcomes by asking students to complete a one-minute paper on what they have learned about searching for news articles using the internet vs. the library discovery tool.

Taste Test:
Can You Tell the Difference Between Library and Google Results?

Kirsten Hostetler, Instruction and Outreach Faculty Librarian, Central Oregon Community College, khostetler@cocc.edu

NUTRITION INFORMATION

Google searches can be a familiar way of finding resources. Students have become accustomed to this interface and can have a difficult time translating those searches to work in libraries' discovery services. This session takes what students already know to act as an introduction to the library's discovery tool.

Learning Outcomes

Students will be able to:

- Compare a Google search to a library discovery tool's search in order to recognize similarities and differences.
- Effectively search the library's discovery tool and recognize various formats of information and its value.

NUMBER SERVED

Serves any number of students.

COOKING TIME

Prep: 10 minutes
Lesson Delivery: 25 minutes

DIETARY GUIDELINES

Frame 1: Information Creation as a Process

Knowledge Practices:

- Assess the fit between an information product's creation process and a particular information need.
- Develop, in their own creation processes, an understanding that their choices impact the purposes for which the information product will be used and the message it conveys.

Dispositions:

- Value the process of matching an information need with an appropriate product.
- Understand that different methods of information dissemination with different purposes are available for their use.

Frame 2: Searching as Strategic Exploration

Knowledge Practices:

- Match information needs and search strategies to appropriate search tools.
- Manage searching processes and results effectively.

Dispositions:

- Realize that information sources vary greatly in content and format and have varying relevance and value, depending on the needs and nature of the search.

- Seek guidance from experts, such as librarians, researchers, and professionals.

INGREDIENTS & EQUIPMENT

- Computer stations for students
- Handout with suggested topics and formats

PREPARATION

- The instructor will prepare a list of topics and item formats (book, article, etc.) for searching.
- It is recommended that the instructor conduct searches prior to class on the internet and in the discovery tool to ensure students will find appropriate results.

COOKING METHOD

1. Explain the session's goals: students will be introduced to the library's discovery tool and learn how they can adapt the search methods they already use to explore library resources. Instructor will give a brief demonstration of the discovery tool by searching with keywords and filtering by format and subject.
2. Students then individually go head-to-head with the instructor to see who can find relevant results faster. For the next five minutes, the instructor will call on

students to find resources on a subject in a particular format using their preferred search engine (it doesn't have to be Google!).

3. The instructor will perform the same search using the discovery tool. Students can see in real time how each search compares. They will then have an opportunity for group discussion to compare the number of results, the ease of filtering by format/subject and the discovery of items relevant to their topic. For example, a student searches Google for a book on Alexander Hamilton while the instructor does the search using the discovery tool.

4. Students then break into groups of two to conduct searches for provided topics and formats in a search engine and in the discovery tool. To ensure both students in each group have the opportunity to search both interfaces, after five minutes have the groups switch from one to the other.

5. Students will then reconvene to discuss the results as a class.

ALLERGY WARNINGS

Students have a hard time volunteering when they are first asked to compare their search to the instructor's. It's often best to call on students and after a few times more students are relaxed enough to volunteer.

CHEF'S NOTE

This recipe can be a great way of meeting students where they are in terms of how

they search in their everyday lives while highlighting what makes a discovery tool different and, ultimately, useful. This activity often leads to a discussion on how information is created and disseminated and how this impacts where they search. Prepare to have a conversation about the differences between item formats and the values of each.

2. THE LARDER
short activities to have on hand

What's in Your Discovery Layer?:
An Introduction to Format

Lisa Eggebraaten, Humanities Librarian, North Dakota State University, lisa.eggebraaten@ndsu.edu; Beth Twomey, Head, Research and Instruction, North Dakota State University, beth.twomey@ndsu.edu

NUTRITION INFORMATION

The purpose of this activity is to introduce students to the "Information Creation as a Process" frame using the variety of resources retrieved from a discovery layer. Students are asked to use a discovery layer record to determine the format of a specific resource. This activity prompts a discussion about how and for what purpose resources were created. Through this activity students will be able to identify different formats, the process that leads to their creation and how to determine if resources are appropriate to use for a given assignment.

Learning Outcomes
Students will be able to:
- Identify a resource's format from the information in the record.
- Explain why a resource type would be acceptable for a given assignment.

NUMBER SERVED
20 to 30 students

COOKING TIME
Preparation is 15 to 20 minutes. Length of lesson is approximately 20 minutes.

DIETARY GUIDELINES
Frame: Information Creation as a Process

Knowledge Practice:
Assess the fit between an information product's creation process and a particular information need.

Disposition:
Inclined to seek out characteristics of information products that indicate the underlying creation process.

INGREDIENTS & EQUIPMENT
- Computer and projector
- PowerPoint slides
- Handouts

PREPARATION
- Select and print out records from the discovery layer prior to the instruction (lamination is an option if they will be used many times).
- Transform records into a PowerPoint presentation and store on a flash drive (if needed).
- Print out assessment sheets.

COOKING METHOD
1. Begin by asking students what happens when they search for "black jacket" (or other generic item) on Amazon. Since most students have used Amazon, students are able to confidently engage in a discussion about how they narrow their searches and make decisions about what jacket would meet their needs. This conversation then switches to the discovery layer and the similarities between it and Amazon.
2. The instructor can bring up the concept that, just like in Amazon, the search results in a discovery layer will not all "fit". They may not be the correct format or have the content they need for their assignment.
3. Briefly introduce the activity: students will examine the discovery layer record for evidence of what type of format it is.
4. Divide students into groups of two to three and distribute a handout to each group. Small group discussions should last no more than a few minutes.
5. Ask each group to report back on what they found. Encourage them to identify the resource and explain their reasoning.

6. As students talk about their record, display the corresponding record on a screen using the PowerPoint slides.
7. Use this opportunity to talk about the different format identifiers found in the discovery layer records, discuss the publishing cycle of different types of publications and the process of peer-review.

ALLERGY WARNINGS
Make handouts that show the greatest variety of formats possible, as well as enough handouts so that students can work in groups of no more than three people.

CHEF'S NOTES
When we first switched to our discovery tool, we found that the number of results overwhelmed students and they assumed that everything retrieved was a physical item held by the library. We developed this lesson for the first-year composition course to engage students with their search results and encourage them to reflect on the variety of information processes that go into the resources they use.

CLEAN UP
The assessment sheet should have a new citation on it. Use a record that presents format information in a different way, such as a Google Scholar item description or a full item citation, to see if students are able to transfer and apply what they learned about discovery layer records in the lesson plan activity. Hand out the assessment and

ask students to circle and name two format identifiers. Have a slide prepared with the citation on it to discuss answers after collecting the assessment.

Short Order Citations Relay

Jennifer Fuller, Assistant Lecturer, English & Philosophy Dept., Idaho State University, fulljen3@isu.edu; Catherine Gray, Coordinator of Library Services, Idaho State University, graycath@isu.edu

NUTRITION INFORMATION

Students often find citations tedious and remark that they all look the same. This recipe allows college freshman students in a second semester composition course to locate sources in the discovery tool and cook up a variety of citations quickly, giving them practice in the different parts that make up citations while also allowing them to see how different materials require different formats. This is a follow-up activity after students have been taught citation elements and styles by the course instructor during a regular class session and had library instruction on the use of databases to locate sources. While designed for first year students, this exercise will also provide important review for upper level students.

Learning Outcomes

Students will be able to:

- Recognize the citation elements of various sources and develop citations in MLA or comparable format.

NUMBER SERVED

Serves an average class of 25 composition students (but can be doubled or halved to suit your needs).

COOKING TIME

Prep time: approximately 90 minutes to locate sources for 25 students (one per student). Depending on how familiar students are with basic discovery tool search techniques, citation styles, and the size of your class, this lesson plan can serve as a 20 to 30 minute refresher or can fill a full class period if students are placed in teams.

DIETARY GUIDELINES

Frame 1: Information Creation as a Process

Knowledge Practice:
Recognize that information may be perceived differently based on the format in which it is packaged.

Dispositions:

- Value the process of matching an information need with an appropriate product.
- Accept that the creation of information may begin initially through communicating in a range of formats or modes.

Frame 2: Information has Value

Knowledge Practices:

- Give credit to the original ideas of others through proper attribution and citation.
- Decide where and how their information is published.

Dispositions:

- Respect the original ideas of others.
- See themselves as contributors to the information marketplace rather than only consumers of it.

INGREDIENTS & EQUIPMENT

- unique citable document for each student team
- citation manuals or citation aids, paper, and pen/pencil (or electronic tablets to pass around)

PREPARATION

Using the library discovery tool, the instructor should retrieve a variety of sources (enough for one per student) and print off the full text (or first few pages) or the title page of each source. These could include a chapter from an edited book, a novel, a reproduction of a work of art, an academic journal, magazine or other source formats that students often use that are included in their citation guides. One set may be easily developed and used each term for multiple classes. The greatest benefit for the student is achieved when the sources are similar with slight variations (a book with one author, three or more authors, an editor, etc.). Have correct citations and assessments prepared before class so you can quickly check the class's answers and address questions.

COOKING METHOD

1. The instructor reviews how to use a citation manual and locate an example for the appropriate source format. Depending on the class's familiarity with citations, instructors may wish to walk through a representative example.

2. Review how a discovery tool can be used to find a wide range of useful sources. As you demonstrate locating sources, point out the different formats, and the facets used to focus the results on specific formats, subject areas, dates of publication, etc.

3. Explain that each student will receive a unique source, different from any other in the class. It will be essential for them to determine the format of each source, and locate the appropriate section in their citation guide before proceeding. Students will fill in the required information until they use a specified punctuation (a period, comma, colon, or italics).

4. Students will then pass their source to the next student, so eventually all students will see all sources as they are rotated. Make sure to explain where the student at the end of the row and the back of the class should pass his or her material. Students will be racing against the clock to finish citations. Prizes will be awarded based on how long it takes the class to finish their citations (the faster the finish, the better the reward). If students are waiting for a partner to finish, they may offer assistance. Instructors should also go to students that are struggling.

5. As students finish, place correctly completed citations in one pile and those with errors into another. Any student in the class may help correct citations with errors until all citations are correct.

Variations

- For larger classes, students can be divided into teams of five to seven students, with each student having a source which will be passed around the team. The first team that completes all the citations correctly would win.

- Additional formats of materials may be provided for students, such as videos, poetry, paintings, sculpture, musical performance, etc. These can be distributed and passed around for the team to develop citations.

ALLERGY WARNINGS

A considerable amount of prep is required for your first cooking session, but materials can be easily reused. Remind students that the goal is to work together to produce efficient and correct citations, not to bully or badger slower moving students. Encourage cheering, conversation, and scorekeeping (15/25 citations complete) beyond just a countdown clock to keep students engaged and motivated. You may also wish to seat quieter students next to more assertive students to avoid potential bottlenecks.

CHEF'S NOTE

Students often begin awkwardly and look slightly terrified. However, as the game continues, students find themselves increasingly comfortable using the citation guide and turning to others for help. By mastering a variety of sources, students have told me they feel like they both understand how citations work and feel confident in their ability to cite any source that they find. Instead of seeing all sources simply as books or articles, students begin to look for nuance and produce far more accurate citations on later paper assignments. Students may also be asked to provide in-text citations for additional practice. Keep in mind, it's important to be aware of students who feel stressed by competition and make sure to provide support to keep the activity feeling like a game rather than an exam.

CLEAN UP

Discuss what students learned during the process, which citations proved especially difficult, and how they felt themselves improving as time went on. Remind students that citation manuals are important tools for their research success, and that there are many difficult sources that warrant using them, even for the most advanced researcher. Have students identify which elements were common to multiple citations and where citations differ.

Goldilocks and the Three Searches:
Learning the Judicious Use of Quotation Marks in Effective Searching

Katie Greer, Assistant Professor, Fine and Performing Arts Librarian, Oakland University, greer@oakland.edu

NUTRITION INFORMATION

The use of quotations has been a difficult concept for students at our university to master, so during one-shot sessions we use the following activity to help illustrate when and how to use them in search strategies. First-year students in the required writing course attend a library session that instructs them on information literacy skills using the library's discovery tool. We recently incorporated the following activity, which utilizes the powerful searching of the discovery tool to illustrate the use of quotation marks as a search strategy. The large number of resources discovery tools retrieve can be overwhelming, providing an opportunity for librarians to teach best practices using a "Goldilocks" style approach, as with the eponymous literary character's trials, to find a combination of search terms that results in a "just right" set of results: not too big and not too small.

Learning Outcomes
Students will be able to:
- Determine when search terms should include quotation marks.
- Demonstrate the use of quotation marks to efficiently and effectively refine discovery tool search results.

NUMBER SERVED
As many as possible

COOKING TIME
This activity can function as a short, five-minute demonstration and discussion, or it can be expanded to include hands-on exploration of the concepts.

DIETARY GUIDELINES
Frame: Searching as Strategic Exploration

Knowledge Practices:
- Utilize divergent (e.g., brainstorming) and convergent (e.g., selecting the best source) thinking when searching.
- Design and refine needs and search strategies as necessary, based on search results;
- manage searching processes and results effectively.

Dispositions:
- Understand that first attempts at searching do not always produce adequate results.
- Persist in the face of search challenges, and know when they have enough information to complete the information task.

INGREDIENTS & EQUIPMENT
- Screen demonstration software, or projector for instructor's computer
- Computers for student use
- Whiteboard or word-processor document for brainstorming

PREPARATION
Have a set of sample research topics that can be used for demonstration purposes and as examples for students to use. The topics should include topical phrases that can be used to demonstrate the use of quotation marks (Figure 1).

COOKING METHOD
1. First, a topic is generated, either through discussion or through pre-selection. In our library, the current sample research question is, "How does screen time impact child development?" The librarian first writes the sample research question on a board or in a projected document, and asks students to pick out the main topical words or phrases. The students then brainstorm a list of potential synonyms or related topical terms for each of the selected terms to try out in a discovery tool search.
2. In our example, the use of the undefined "screen time" in the sample

question provides an opportunity for students to suggest and discuss the effect of broader or narrower terms when formulating searches, eg: computer, tablet, television, media, etc. Similarly, "impact" is discussed in terms of what synonyms might contain bias (benefit, delay). Once a list of potential terms and phrases has been generated, the librarian explains the function of quotations in a search strategy. The librarian then demonstrates what we call the "Goldilocks approach" to searching using quotation marks: a process to find the combination of terms and quotation marks which lead to results that are not too big, not too small, but "just right."

3. Not enough quotations can lead to results which are too big. A sample search is conducted that does not utilize quotations to isolate phrases. The results are overwhelmingly numerous: in our discovery tool, using the sample question above, a search for [screen time impact child development] leads to over 250,000 results.

4. Quotations used inappropriately lead to results which are too small. We demonstrate an erroneous tactic that we often see from students: putting the quotations around the entire search: "screen time impact child development". This leads to zero results.

5. Lastly, a search is demonstrated which uses quotations in appropriate places. This leads to results which are "just right." By using quotation marks judi-

FIGURE 1. Topics and Keywords Sample
Sample topic: *How does screen time impact child development?*

Research topic or question:		
Search Conducted	**Number of Results**	**Relevant Results? Other Comments?**

ciously, the results list becomes more manageable, especially as the class goes on to discuss the use of limits and other search strategies. Our example search, ["screen time" impact "child development"] results in just over 700 items.

6. After the demonstration, the class is given time to try out using quotations. Some classes come in with their own research topics and are encouraged to use those so that the librarian can answer any questions they have. Classes which do not yet have research assignments experiment using the terms and phrases which were brainstormed during the activity, or a sample topic of their choosing.

7. This time can be structured as a think-pair-share activity or as individual work with the librarian checking in on every-

one. If used as a think-pair-share, then in pairs or small groups the students define a search strategy using quotations and then test it out, refining as necessary. A worksheet which provides a table for notes on searching strategies is helpful for the activity (Figure 1). After about 5 minutes of practice, the students report back to the class on their topic, their search strategy, and what they found successful and any problems they encountered.

ALLERGY WARNINGS

It's helpful to emphasize that the use of quotations is for terms and phrases instead of single keywords. Students occasionally continue to do this even after the discussion and practice. Sample topics which involve proper names also illustrate this concept well.

CHEF'S NOTE

The use of quotations has been such a thorny issue that we have continued to expand upon and develop new strategies for teaching it and putting it into active learning. The Goldilocks approach, with its connection to the well-known folktale, allows for a more enjoyable presentation and a more meaningful and engaged student experience.

CLEAN UP

Formative assessment can be provided during the discussion and search demonstrations as the librarian solicits feedback on search formation and results. Questions such as, "why do you think this search led to this number of results" or "what is the purpose of quotation marks in this example" can be used to reinforce concepts and generate further questions or insights from the students. During the active learning portion of the class, the student presentations, if done as a think-pair-share activity, provide opportunities for the librarian or the class as a whole to talk about what went well and why, or what could be changed to be more effective. If students are working individually on their various projects, the librarian can assess how well students understood the concepts presented when talking to each student about the search terms and quotation strategies being used.

If the class is online, modules which explain the use of quotation marks can include assessment throughout. Our online version of the first-year instruction, housed within the university's learning management system, includes "test your understanding" questions in the content modules and questions on the final quiz that ask students to choose where quotation marks should be placed given a sample set of topic search terms.

Finding a Recipe by Ingredients

Olga Hart, Coordinator of Library Instruction, University of Cincinnati, olga.hart@uc.edu

NUTRITION INFORMATION

In this activity students learn to locate full text from citations through small group work, demonstrations, and discussions. If desired, citation formats could be explored (why they exist and why they are different).

Learning Outcomes

Students will be able to:

- Interpret citations in order to successfully use a discovery tool to locate cited sources.
- Locate the full text of an item either online or in print and request items from the library system, consortium, or via interlibrary loan.
- Understand that desired information is not always available online and be able to articulate possible reasons for access limitations.

NUMBER SERVED

Any class size; I worked with groups of 10 to 25.

COOKING TIME

Preparation: 30 minutes, "prepared ingredients" can be saved and reused.
Cooking: 5 minutes for small group work and 10 to 15 minutes for presentations depending on the class size. Allow time for follow-up discussions.

DIETARY GUIDELINES

Frame 1: Information Has Value

Knowledge Practices:

- Give credit to the original ideas of others through proper attribution and citation.
- Recognize issues of access or lack of access to information sources.

Disposition:
Respect the original ideas of others.

Frame 2: Searching as Strategic Exploration

Knowledge Practice:
Match information needs and search strategies to appropriate search tools.

Disposition:
Persist in the face of search challenges, and know when they have enough information to complete the information task.

INGREDIENTS & EQUIPMENT

- Computer classroom
- Citations to a variety of sources (see details under "Preparation") on cards or slips of paper. Make enough cards for groups of 2 to 3 students (you will need 8 to 10 for a group of 25; the same citation may be used more than once)
- A list of all citations in a Word document to project on the screen
- Box or basket (optional)

PREPARATION

- Select citations to sources that are likely to be used in the course/assignment.
- Print the citations on cards or slips of paper.
- Arrange them as a fan, or put them into a box or basket to distribute in class. Each citation is preceded with the following questions: What type of material (book, article, etc.) is represented by the following citation? How would you get full text?

COOKING METHOD

1. Begin the class by discussing the importance of being able to find a source for which they have a citation. For example, they may want to locate a chapter listed in their course readings or an article cited in a source they used for their paper.
2. Divide the class into small groups and have each group select a citation you prepared in advance of class.
3. Point the students to the discovery tool. Each group has five minutes to determine what type of material is represented by the citation and locate the full

text, which may or may not be available online. At this point I do not provide any tips on using the discovery tool – students share them in their mini-presentations or I do so in conclusion.

4. Groups or their assigned representatives present in front of the class. First, they state what material type is represented by the citation and the class has a chance to agree or disagree. It helps students to hear the reasoning provided by their peers. Some students are better than others paying attention to details such as volume and issue number, pages ranges, etc.

5. Next, the students show the steps they used to locate the resource (complete or partial citation, use of the advanced interface, etc.).

6. Students show how they were able to find the full text of the item or information that would help them get it, such as a call number for a book or the Interlibrary Loan form for articles not available online. If a group's search turned out unsuccessful, invite suggestions from class.

7. Provide comments and suggestions if students are "stuck" or fail to mention something important.

8. Talk about additional tools that might be useful in locating cited sources, such as the library catalog, Google, Google Books, and Google Scholar. When talking about the latter mention that the version retrieved on the internet may not be the final published version.

ALLERGY WARNINGS

This recipe is allergy-free; it's great for any type of audience.

CHEF'S NOTE

Conversations resulting from this activity might address one or more of the following issues: limitations of databases; rights to full text; access to licensed resources; difference between citation formats in various disciplines; or selection of tools depending on search need.

CLEAN UP

In this activity students demonstrate their ability to interpret citations and locate cited sources, so the assessment is instant. Authentic assessment takes place in the course when students need to apply this ability. If the librarian is embedded in the course, (s)he may observe the application by responding to students' questions on locating cited sources or having online discussions.

Library Discovery and Draw

Kirsten Hostetler, Instruction and Outreach Faculty Librarian, Central Oregon Community College, khostetler@cocc.edu

NUTRITION INFORMATION

For most students, a library tour or orientation is their first experience with a college library, post-high school or after a period of absence from school. While it is important to introduce students to the physical library space, we would be remiss not to include some introduction to online resources and services during these sessions. This recipe gives students a chance to engage creatively with the library's discovery tool and sparks conversations about what resources attract students' attention and why.

Learning Outcomes

Students will be able to:
- Recognize essential elements of the library's discovery tool.
- Effectively search the library's discovery tool using their knowledge of the tool's components and layout.

NUMBER SERVED

Serves any number of students, but smaller groups are more manageable

COOKING TIME

Prep time: 5 minutes
Lesson delivery: 20 minutes

DIETARY GUIDELINES

Frame: Searching as Strategic Exploration

Knowledge Practices:
- Utilize divergent (e.g., brainstorming) and convergent (e.g., selecting the best source) thinking when searching.
- Understand how information systems (i.e., collections of recorded information) are organized in order to access relevant information.

Dispositions:
- Exhibit mental flexibility and creativity.
- Realize that information sources vary greatly in content and format and have varying relevance and value, depending on the needs and nature of the search.

INGREDIENTS & EQUIPMENT
- Computer stations for students
- Blank paper
- Writing tools
- White board

PREPARATION

As this lesson plan requires students to take the instructional lead, the only preparation is ensuring you have enough blank paper and writing tools as well as selecting keywords for the students' searches.

COOKING METHOD

1. Explain the session's goals: Students will be introduced to the library's discovery tool with their peers taking the instructional lead. Explain what a discovery tool is.
2. Break the students into groups of two. If there are uneven groups, one student can be an observer and take notes. One student will face the computer and the other will sit facing away from the computer.
3. Have the student facing the computer navigate to the library's discovery tool with the instructor's guidance. The student will do a search using keywords the instructor wrote on the whiteboard.
4. The student will then describe the results page of the discovery tool to the student who cannot see the screen.
5. Based on their peer's description, the student partners will draw the library's discovery tool. They have five minutes to complete their illustration.
6. Students may now turn around to see the screen and compare it to their drawing. Allow the groups a few minutes to discuss the results amongst themselves before sharing with the class.
7. The remaining time is spent discussing the layout of the discovery tool and what the different sections, as high-

lighted in the drawings, are used for. Instructors can guide the conversation to discover what students thought were the most prominent features and why they think the library would choose to highlight those tools.

8. Inevitably, students will be interested in certain areas over others, so each drawing will be more accurate for specific sections. Using each of the students' drawings, you can call attention to the different sections of the discovery tool—filtering options, citation tools, etc.—and explain how they are used. This is a lighthearted way to show students where resources are (which they covered by explaining or drawing the tool), and what they are used for (which is covered in the discussion).

your discovery tool so you know what they are drawn to (so to speak) and what they overlook.

ALLERGY WARNINGS

Students will need to be encouraged to think creatively and be active participants in the conversation. The room can get loud as students excitedly describe what they see on their computer screen.

CHEF'S NOTE

This session is definitely not the standard lecture. It allows students to think creatively and can be a helpful icebreaker. There are usually some miscommunications or non-artistically-inclined students that spark some humor. Students tend to enjoy the reveal of their classmates' drawings the most. This recipe has the added bonus of getting student feedback on the usability of

Scavenging for Research Ingredients

Jessica Hronchek, Research and Instruction Librarian, Hope College, hronchek@hope.edu

NUTRITION INFORMATION

First-year students are asked to compete in a scavenger hunt using their library's discovery tool. By participating in this guided seek and find activity, they will be introduced to key features and search strategies for the platform and have the opportunity to practice them.

Learning Outcomes
Students will be able to:
- Perform simple effective keyword searches in a discovery tool.
- Locate relevant sources on a pre-defined topic.
- Choose discovery tool limiters to refine their searches.

NUMBER SERVED

Serves 15 to 30

COOKING TIME

Prep time: 30 minutes to 1 hour
Lesson delivery: 15 to 30 minutes, depending on the number of questions created

DIETARY GUIDELINES

Frame: Searching as Strategic Exploration

Knowledge Practices:
- Design and refine needs and search strategies as necessary, based on search results.

- Manage searching processes and results effectively.

Dispositions:
Understand that first attempts at searching do not always produce adequate results.

INGREDIENTS & EQUIPMENT
- One computer for every two to three students.
- Instructor computer station
- Scavenger hunt worksheets, one copy for each group
- Small prize for the winning group (we use library promotional items)

PREPARATION

Identify the features of your discovery platform that you want your students exposed to and create a worksheet of scavenger hunt questions that highlight these features. For example, ask students to answer a question (report number of search results) or locate a specific item (peer-reviewed journal article on a specific topic). At the end of the worksheet, give students instructions on how to e-mail their answers to the librarian using the discovery tool's folder/list function. If your platform includes an embedded citation tool that you wish to highlight, ask students to send their answers in a specified citation style.

FIGURE 1. Discovery Tool Scavenger Hunt

1. Pick a team name.
2. How many results do you get when you search: **peace AND sports**?
3. How many results do you get when you search **peace AND sports diplomacy**?
4. Find an article on this topic in a *peer reviewed journal*. Save it to your folder.
5. Find an article or book on this topic published between 2000 and 2008. Add it to your folder.
6. Find a book about politics and the Olympics written by **Kay Schaffer**. (**Hint**: the advanced search features appears if you click the wheel next to the search button, and you will find a way to search by author here).
7a. How many results do you get when you search **Olympic boycott 1980**?
7b. How many do you get searching **"Olympic boycott" 1980**?
7c. Based on what you see, what purpose do quotation marks have in a search?

To Complete the Scavenger Hunt
Go to your folder of saved items and e-mail your list of resources to me (insert your e-mail address here). **ALSO**, in the message box, type in your team name and the answers you found to questions 2, 3 and 7(a–c). First group to submit the worksheet with the most correct answers gets a prize!

COOKING METHOD

1. Show students how to get to the discovery tool on the library's website. Briefly introduce the discovery platform as an entry point to many of your library's resources. Avoid a lengthy lecture, as this is intended to be a hands-on exploratory exercise. Explain that, rather than watching a demonstration, they will be exploring the tool for themselves through a scavenger hunt.

2. Divide the class into groups of two to three students, with a computer and a worksheet for each group (Figure 1).

3. If the discovery platform requires a login to collect items to a folder, have one member of each group create an account.

4. Before they start, give them a couple of tips for completing the exercise. For example, show them the folder/list feature for saving items. Briefly point out the limiting features as a way to narrow their searches.

5. Mention that there will be a prize for the group that submits their answers with the most speed and accuracy.

6. As the groups work through the scavenger hunt, work the room and answer questions and provide hints if students seem overly stuck. Monitor your e-mail for group submissions, encouraging all groups to submit their answers as winners will be selected by both speed *and* accuracy.

7. Check the answers as they come in and select a winning team. The winner is the group that submitted the worksheet with the most correct answers first.

ALLERGY WARNINGS

The activity as designed requires students to e-mail folders of resources to the librarian in order to submit their scavenger hunt answers. Have students create a team name so that you can identify each group. If you want them to provide text answers to certain questions, then your discovery system will need to have a "comments" or "notes" box that they can use to do this. If your system does not have this, consider an alternate method for submitting answers or limit to item-based answers.

CHEF'S NOTE

I encourage this to be a competitive activity. Students are much more engaged with the scavenger hunt when they knew they are working against other teams. There are many features that you can demonstrate through this exercise; in the past I have focused on concise keyword searching and narrowing, Boolean searching, using quotation marks, narrowing by date range, locating specific material types, and finding resources by specific authors. Also, this is a good activity to use for courses with multiple sections. I was able to tweak the worksheet from section to section based on the areas in which students struggled.

CLEAN UP

Use the submitted answers to identify skills and concepts that are unclear to the students. End the exercise by clarifying the muddy points while demonstrating a search.

Cooking Up Keywords

Grace Kaletski, Learning & Information Literacy Librarian, Stetson University, gkaletsk@stetson.edu

NUTRITION INFORMATION

Use this activity to help students think creatively to identify keywords and synonyms on their research topic. Each student will record their research question on a worksheet and use the library's discovery tool to find keyword synonyms for their topic. Next, students will be asked to share with the class the specific strategies they used to find keywords. Finally, the librarian will point out any strategies students may have overlooked.

Learning Outcomes

Students will be able to:
- Understand the concept of a keyword and select syntax that a discovery tool can process.
- Discover keywords and synonyms relevant to a topic within the discovery tool interface.
- Use advanced features of the library discovery tool.

NUMBER SERVED

This activity may work with a class of any size.

COOKING TIME

Prep time: can vary between 15 to 60 minutes
Lesson delivery: 30 minutes

DIETARY GUIDELINES

Frame: Searching as Strategic Exploration

Knowledge Practices:
- Understand how information systems (i.e., collections of recorded information) are organized to access relevant information.
- Use different types of searching language e.g., controlled vocabulary, keywords, natural language) appropriately.

Dispositions:
- Exhibit mental flexibility and creativity.
- Understand that first attempts at searching do not always produce adequate results.

INGREDIENTS & EQUIPMENT

- Projector and enough computers for each student. If a sufficient number of computers is not available, students may work in groups or pairs.

PREPARATION

- Contact the course instructor to identify any course assignments that require library research and determine what stage of the project students will be in at the time information literacy instruction takes place.
- Secure space for instruction that provides access to all of the necessary equipment.
- Create or tweak a worksheet that provides space for students to record

their research question, keywords, and synonyms.
- Students should come to class prepared with a topic or research question.

COOKING METHOD

1. Pass out worksheets (Figure 1) and have students record their research question.
2. Briefly introduce the discovery tool and the concept of keywords. Ask students to list the keywords they would use to find information on their topic on the worksheet.
3. Ask students to find creative ways to use the discovery tool to come up with synonyms for their keywords, and challenge them not to use outside sources (e.g. Google, Wikipedia). Point out general places in the discovery tool where synonyms might be hidden, such as the panel of refinement options, item records, or the full text of results.
4. Avoid telling students specifically where to get synonyms at this point in the lesson, although stronger hints may be necessary if you walk around the room and find students who are struggling with the activity. The amount of time required for this independent exploration may vary depending on the class context.

FIGURE 1. Keywords and Synonyms Worksheet

1. Write down your topic or research question. Be specific:

IS A LIBERAL ARTS EDUCATION IMPORTANT?

2. Identify the keywords in your research question (usually the nouns).

LIBERAL ARTS, EDUCATION, IMPORTANT

3. Use the discovery tool to identify synonyms or words you can use as alternatives to your keywords. Be creative—think outside the (Google) box!

First Keyword	Second Keyword	Third Keyword
LIBERAL ARTS	EDUCATION	IMPORTANT
HUMANITIES	HIGHER EDUCATION	VALUE
ARTS AND SCIENCES	LEARNING	VALUABLE
LITERATURE	CURRICULUM	USEFUL
CRITICAL THINKING	COLLEGE	BENEFIT
NON-STEM	UNIVERSITY	PURPOSE

learning experience. Some students may try to jump ahead and fill out the worksheet as soon as they write down the research question, so it may be wise to discourage this before the discovery tool is introduced.

CHEF'S NOTE
This lesson is based on the principles of problem-based learning and active learning. This activity provides a great segue into Boolean searching.

CLEAN UP
Formative assessment takes place when students are asked to share the strategies used to find keywords and synonyms. Collecting worksheets and reviewing them after class is a great way to implement summative assessment, but make sure to coordinate with the instructor to get the worksheets back to students later. Alternatively, if technology is available, a web form that can be submitted to the librarian and saved for the student can be used instead of a worksheet.

5. Turn students' attention back to the class. Ask if anyone was able to find synonyms for their topic. Then, ask students to volunteer to describe or demonstrate for their classmates any strategies they used to successfully find keyword synonyms with the discovery tool.

6. The librarian can elaborate on student strategies and share ideas that are not mentioned, such using encyclopedia entries, subject headings, abstracts, author-supplied keywords, etc. to identify synonyms.

ALLERGY WARNINGS
This activity is most useful when students already have a research question. Be prepared to adjust if students are researching for a group project, in which case this lesson could be used as a group activity instead. Even if there is not a group project, encouraging collaboration while students are searching for synonyms may enrich the

When There's No Time to Cook, but There's a Guest at Your House, Keep Something in the Freezer You Can Pop in the Oven

Christina Riehman-Murphy, Reference and Instruction Librarian, Penn State University, Abington Campus, cer20@psu.edu

NUTRITION INFORMATION

This recipe isn't a recipe at all! It's the box of pizza bites you keep in the fridge when your son's friends come over to study after school but then casually mention they're starving and they just can't study until they eat something.

It's what often happens in your one-shot library instruction. You've e-mailed with the professor who sent you the assignment for their six to eight page research essay and what (s)he was looking for in your class. Usually it's an overview of library resources and a demonstration of databases that will be helpful for the students to answer their research questions. The professor is hoping they'll leave your class with some good quality sources. You've prepared your lesson plan and your handouts and your search demonstrations.

On the day of, you begin the class, introduce yourself, and then ask if any of the students are willing to share their research questions. You mention as an incentive that if they do share it, you'll do a sample search around it. A few hands go up and when you call on them, you hear a series of responses that go like this: "I'm doing my paper on… gun violence… Greece… teen pregnancy… homosexuality." For each one of those students, you ask them to narrow it down: "What about gun violence do you plan on writing about?" And each student sort of shrugs.

That's when you realize they will get little out of this instruction because they don't really have research questions or topics for their essay. They need to narrow their ideas down. So you pull out your post-it note pad.

Learning Outcomes

Students will be able to:

- Narrow their topics by discovering new concepts and the relationships between them.
- Perform efficient and organized information searches that enhance their knowledge of their topics.

NUMBER SERVED

Up to 25, but the recipe could easily be adjusted to any number of students (just bring an extra post-it pad).

COOKING TIME

Prep time: 5 minutes is all you need
Cooking time: 15 minutes at the most. You want to just introduce the tool and set them on the path to using it as they search. If they like it, they will use it as they search and take it with them when they go.

DIETARY GUIDELINES

Frame: Searching as Strategic Exploration

Knowledge Practice:
Design and refine needs and search strategies as necessary, based on search results.

Disposition:
- Exhibit mental flexibility and creativity.
- Recognize the value of browsing and other serendipitous methods of information gathering.

INGREDIENTS & EQUIPMENT

This is one-ingredient cooking! All you need is one 4x6 post-it pad. It's preferable if students have their own computers, but it can easily be done just through the librarian's demonstration of the task.

PREPARATION

Grab a marker and your post-it pad. Spend five minutes drawing ovals in the middle of each sheet. Keep your ovals around an inch. It's enough room to write just one or two words. This helps guide students into thinking about keywords or concepts instead of typing entire questions or phrases into the discovery tool.

COOKING METHOD

1. Hand out one post-it sheet to each student.
2. Ask them to write their topics in the oval. Tell them they can write no more than two words.
3. Have them draw four lines coming from their first oval and draw an oval at the end of each of those lines.
4. Students then open their laptops, go to the discovery tool homepage, and type the words from their oval into the discovery tool.
5. Students must scan results for two minutes before they write anything else down on their sticky note. Encourage them to search through at least two pages of results.
6. Time it!
7. When two minutes are up, ask them to write down four particular aspects of their topic that they discovered in their search that they found interesting (Figure 1). Again, limit them to no more than two words in each oval. For example, if football was a student's original topic, after they scanned the results in the discovery tool then might add concussions or paid athletes to their ovals.
8. Now ask them to circle the one branch that they are most interested in.
9. Have them move on to using the advanced search feature. This time they should use their center oval term(s) in the first box and put their next oval term in the second box. The discovery tool helps them understand that there are hundreds of different ways to approach their topics with different arguments to be made around each of those aspects. Often times they start to narrow their topics even further.

ALLERGY WARNINGS

While this is simply teaching the students to concept map, I've found that the less jargon used, the better. Also, it's important to use sticky pads! Tell them to stick theirs to their handouts when they leave.

FIGURE 1. Topic Example

CHEF'S NOTE

The great thing about this ready-to-go recipe is that although it's just a simple concept map, it helps them narrow their topics, provides a search strategy, introduces the idea of searching using keywords, and makes them take notes. When the class period is a bit longer, I like to give each student two sheets. Instead of letting them start with their topics, I guide them through one that I've chosen, before moving on to their own topics.

CLEAN UP

Once students have finished the activity, take a few minutes to implement some formative assessment. I recommend asking at least five students to share the initial topic they began with in their first oval along with its two accompanying sub-ovals to see how they narrowed their topic down after using the discovery tool. Doing this allows the not only the chef, but also the other students to see more examples of the process.

Using Discovery to Facilitate Source Awareness and Evaluation

Rachel Scott, Integrated Library Systems Librarian, University of Memphis, rescott3@memphis.edu

NUTRITION INFORMATION

Discovery tools are great at revealing the cornucopia of sources available for any given topic. This one-shot lesson makes use of discovery platform facets to show students the range of content available. They will also understand how the available information sources differ from each other. The lesson is more appropriate for upper-level students who have research experience and a basic understanding of what research looks like within their disciplines.

Learning Outcomes

Students will be able to:
- Use facets in order to refine searches in the discovery layer.
- Evaluate discovery platform results in order to recognize the variety of published literature on a topic.

NUMBER SERVED

Reservations required! Seating limited to 30.

COOKING TIME

Prep time depends on discovery familiarity; 1 to 2 hours
Lesson delivery: 40 to 60 minutes

DIETARY GUIDELINES

Frame: Searching as Strategic Exploration

Knowledge Practices:
- Understand how information systems (i.e., collections of recorded information) are organized in order to access relevant information.
- Design and refine needs and search strategies as necessary, based on search results.

Dispositions:
- Realize that information sources vary greatly in content and format and have varying relevance and value, depending on the needs and nature of the search.
- Exhibit mental flexibility and creativity.

INGREDIENTS & EQUIPMENT

- Computer classroom with internet access
- Overhead projection for demonstration
- Worksheet

PREPARATION

- Collect an assignment description from the classroom instructor and conduct several searches to test the local discovery platform.
- You may want to plan ahead so the sample searches that you perform retrieve sources which allow you to explain the various facets and features you wish to highlight. Keep in mind,

however, that content is added frequently and results cannot be controlled.
- Customize the worksheet and cooking methods accordingly.

COOKING METHOD

1. Distribute the worksheets (Figure 1) and briefly explain the content and objectives of the class.
2. Begin by demonstrating an assignment-based search in the discovery layer.
3. Discuss the results: What do the icons signify? How can you tell if the source is an article? Can you identify an e-book? What content are we searching right now? Briefly explain the content that is included in the discovery tool. Also, explain relevancy ranking.
4. Next, explain the facets on the left-hand side of the page that will help students refine their search results.
5. Demonstrate the date limiter and discuss why and when one might want to limit to current or historical information.
6. Explain the format facet and ask the class when and why different formats might be preferable. Connect the discussion to a class assignment or project, if possible. Demonstrate limiting by a specific format to show how it reduces the results to a select set of items.

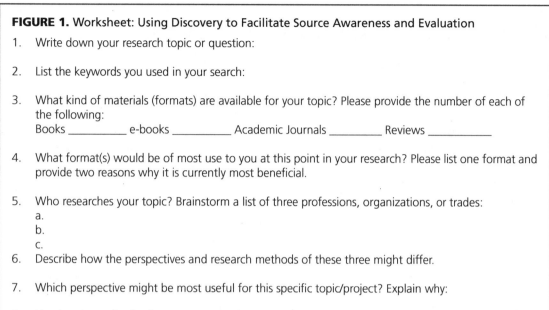

FIGURE 1. Worksheet: Using Discovery to Facilitate Source Awareness and Evaluation

1. Write down your research topic or question:

2. List the keywords you used in your search:

3. What kind of materials (formats) are available for your topic? Please provide the number of each of the following:
    Books _____ e-books _____ Academic Journals _____ Reviews _____

4. What format(s) would be of most use to you at this point in your research? Please list one format and provide two reasons why it is currently most beneficial.

5. Who researches your topic? Brainstorm a list of three professions, organizations, or trades:
    a.
    b.
    c.

6. Describe how the perspectives and research methods of these three might differ.

7. Which perspective might be most useful for this specific topic/project? Explain why:

8. List the name of a database or journal title that you think is written from this perspective:

CHEF'S NOTE

The unique capabilities of discovery platforms and their differences from traditional, hierarchical systems, both in content and organization, have created a need to train librarians and users alike. By teaching skills and promoting reflection, librarians can enrich students' information retrieval practices both in the session and long after.

CLEAN UP

Discuss with the instructor the possibility of grading the worksheet. Some instructors are willing to assign participation, attendance, or extra credit grades, while others may be thrilled to allow the librarian to grade or provide feedback to students.

7. Explain the subject or topic facet. If your class is at a level where you think it is appropriate you can explain subject headings and the lack of a consistent controlled vocabulary in discovery tools.

8. Open the facet of "more databases" to reveal the variety of subject-specific and interdisciplinary databases. Ask which professions might research this topic and which perspectives should be considered for this topic. Demonstrate clicking on a specific database to show how it limits results.

9. Discuss the importance of refining search terms based on the results retrieved. Encourage students to read abstracts and check subject headings to identify additional search terms.

10. Discuss other ways to refine their search such as advanced search options, Boolean operators and using quotation marks for phrases.

11. Use the remaining time to allow students to start working on their worksheet, ask questions, and further familiarize themselves with the discovery platform.

ALLERGY WARNINGS

The recipe may vary based on the particular discovery tool used. Chefs may find it useful to do a dry run of the recipe alone in the kitchen. As you prepare, take care to note inconsistencies and problems and consider reporting these to your vendor or systems librarian. They may be able to give you helpful explanations or resolve the issue.

3. TAPAS
group activities

Keywords to the Rescue: An Essential Side Dish to Spice Up Your Main Meal

Joshua Becker, Information Literacy and Assessment Librarian, Southern New Hampshire University, j.becker3@snhu.edu

NUTRITION INFORMATION

This activity shows students how persistence and creativity can lead to better searches. After this activity, students are empowered to conduct searches on their own.

Each student will generate keywords based on the same topic. Groups of students will discuss their keywords, then search for three to four relevant sources. Each group will briefly share their search strategy for their top finding with the class.

Learning Outcomes

Students will be able to:

- Generate a variety of keywords related to a given topic.
- Use a discovery tool to find sources on their topics.
- Evaluate and select relevant sources from a discovery tool.

NUMBER SERVED

Classes up to 30 students

COOKING TIME

20 to 30 minutes for the lesson; 1 to 2 hours for the preparation

DIETARY GUIDELINES

Frame: Research as Inquiry

Knowledge Practices:
Monitor gathered information and assess for gaps or weaknesses.

Dispositions:

- Consider research as open-ended exploration and engagement with information.
- Value persistence, adaptability, and flexibility and recognize that ambiguity can benefit the research process.

INGREDIENTS & EQUIPMENT

- 3 x 5 index cards (regular lined paper could also work)
- Computers for students
- Instructor station

PREPARATION

- Students should have some previous exposure with databases and discovery tools, and should already know how to conduct a basic search.
- Students should also have a general understanding of scholarly information and how to evaluate sources for relevance and authority.
- A topic relevant to the students' work should be selected in consultation with the course professor. If possible, select a topic where the most obvious keywords yield poor results.

- The librarian should conduct a thorough search using a wide variety of keywords, and should identify some of the most relevant sources that groups are likely to select.

COOKING METHOD

1. Distribute index cards to students. All students are given the same topic to brainstorm.
2. Students will briefly write down as many keywords as they can for that topic.
3. In small groups students will briefly compare and discuss their keywords.
4. Working in these groups, students will search the discovery tool using their keywords to find three to four relevant academic sources on the class topic. A group member will put these sources in the online folder that is part of the tool and e-mails it to the librarian. These folders will record each group's sources, creating a permanent file that can be used by the librarian and course professor.
5. One student from each group will share their chosen keywords and explain how their best source was found and why they consider it the best source. Each group will present for approximately two minutes.

ALLERGY WARNING

In addition to course-related topics, hot topics such as "Should pets be allowed to live on campus?" tend to be a huge hit with students. Small groups of two or three students work best and allow for a meaningful discussion among members and a more interesting variety of chosen sources. Some students like the experience of using the instructor's station to demonstrate their search to the class. In larger classes, time may not permit having every group present.

CHEF'S NOTE

Students often become frustrated when their initial search query yields poor results in discovery tools. By placing them in a low-stakes group environment, students become more familiar with the nuances of the tool. This activity can also be a valuable learning experience for librarians. It's often interesting to find which keywords were chosen and the sources that they yielded.

CLEAN UP

The group folder of three to four sources often serves as the primary assessment for this activity. The librarian will evaluate each folder to determine how effectively groups chose relevant sources. Alternatively, the index cards can be used to establish if the generated keywords were suitable for the research topic.

Teaching Discovery Through Cooperative Learning: A Jigsaw Approach

Robert Farrell, Associate Professor, Library Coordinator of Information Literacy and Assessment, Lehman College, City University of New York, robert.farrell@lehman.cuny.edu

NUTRITION INFORMATION

Teaching students a discovery tool takes the discovery out of Discovery. The goal of this jigsaw-style activity is to empower teams of students to discover how various aspects of a discovery tool function and allow students to teach the other teams what they've learned.

Learning Outcomes

Students will be able to:
- Locate information in a variety of formats using a discovery tool.
- Understand and be able to explain to others aspects of a discovery tool through inquiring into its structure and function.

NUMBER SERVED

6 to 30 students

COOKING TIME

30 minutes plus a one-time, one-hour prep to construct worksheet

DIETARY GUIDELINES

Frame 1: Research as Inquiry

Knowledge Practices:
- Deal with complex research by break-ing complex questions into simple ones, limiting the scope of investigations.
- Use various research methods, based on need, circumstance, and type of inquiry.

Dispositions:
- Consider research as open-ended ex-ploration and engagement with infor-mation.
- Value persistence, adaptability, and flexibility and recognize that ambiguity can benefit the research process.

Frame 2: Searching as Strategic Exploration

Knowledge Practices:
- Determine the initial scope of the task required to meet their information needs.
- Understand how information systems (i.e., collections of recorded informa-tion) are organized in order to access relevant information.

Dispositions:
- Understand that first attempts at searching do not always produce ad-equate results.

- Persist in the face of search challenges, and know when they have enough information to complete the informa-tion task.

INGREDIENTS & EQUIPMENT

- Instructor station with computer, pro-jector and screen or smartboard
- Computers for student use
- Printed activity (one page)

PREPARATION

- Instructor creates a worksheet with six complex questions/problems aimed at getting students to explore different aspects of the discovery tool environ-ment (Figure 1). Topics for exploration are of less importance than the activity of exploring the discovery environment. That said, instructors can select search topics relevant to course subject matter if that is important.

COOKING METHOD

1. Introduction to class: "You will be grouped into teams. Each team will each solve one of the problems on this worksheet. Your team will have 10 to 15 minutes to solve the problem. At the

end of that time, each team will present how you solved your problem. You will be the professors for this part of the session."

2. Instructor groups students into six teams. Pairs are ideal. If working with a large class, two or more pairs can work concurrently on the same problem. Students can work individually in the case of small classes.

3. Teams work to solve their problems for 10 to 15 minutes. The instructor walks around the room during this time, monitoring the progress of the teams and offering guiding questions when needed, being careful not to direct students to the answer or solution. The instructor should aim to guide students toward productively seeing questions or problems in cases where teams seem to have found a quick or easy solution.

4. The instructor reconvenes the class as a group and invites each team to the front of the room (instructor station) at the end of the given time. If more than one team has worked on a problem, each team should be given time to present their solution, with the second team providing supplementation or additional options depending on what they've discovered.

5. If needed, at the end of each team's presentation the instructor can ask the team directed questions to discover more efficient ways of solving the problem. The instructor can also turn to the larger class and ask if they have any ideas on how to supplement or differently approach the problem. Alternately, the instructor can supplement the presented solution or offer an alternative way of solving the problem. Given that a team will have found some sort of solution, it is important not to "correct" the students. Within this learning context, some solutions may be inefficient or less than ideal, but no solution is "wrong."

6. Once a team has finished its presentation and the instructor has supplemented it, the team is applauded and the next team takes their turn.

FIGURE 1. Group Worksheet

Team 1:
Find a physical book about X located somewhere in this library. Where in the library is the book located? How would you find the book on the shelf? Next, find an e-book about X. What's the best way to view this book? Our e-books are only accessible to our students. If you were off-campus, how would you be able to access the book?

Team 2:
Find an article from a newspaper on something related to X. What newspaper is it from? Where did the discovery tool take you to find the article? What's the name of the website? What is this thing?

Team 3:
Do a search for: X. What parts of the discovery tool website are important? What is the function of each part?

Team 4:
Using the discovery tool, do a search for X. How many results did you get? How can you narrow down your results? Think through as many ways as you can to narrow down results.

Team 5:
You live near Yankee Stadium in the Bronx. What is the closest CUNY library to you? How would you find books at the library? How would you have them delivered to Lehman? What would you need to have with you if you wanted to go to that library and check the book out in person?

Team 6:
I'm really interested in X's relationship to Y. Open a peer reviewed journal article. What are the important characteristics of the article? What is a "peer-reviewed journal"? What kinds of articles are published there?

ALLERGY WARNING

The problems posed to the teams are intentionally broad in scope in order to provide students with ample opportunity for independent exploration. Consequently, the instructor may need to offer more guidance to individual teams than others during the problem-solving phase of the activity. For example, Team 3's problem aims at having students visually analyze the discovery tool interface in order to determine the functionality of each section of the page that comes up once results are retrieved.

In the presentation phase, students teach other students where the advanced search button is, where the limiters are, where they can specify material type, etc. The librarian can pose questions to prompt exploration during the problem solving phase as needed or wait to ask questions during or after the presentation phase that direct students to notice and explain features of the tool they may have missed.

CHEF'S NOTE

While the jigsaw approach has been used in a variety of learning contexts, this use of the activity has been taught by the author as part of a larger 75 minute, freshman-level session inspired by ideas from critical theorist Jacques Ranciere's work in the area of critical pedagogy.

The session draws on two ideas from Ranciere's book *The Ignorant Schoolmaster* (Ranciere, 1991): 1) that the best instructor is the one who does not necessarily know the subject matter being taught, but the one who best directs the attention of students toward asking and answering increasingly complex questions; 2) that we can choose to consider all human beings as possessing the same ability to learn and thereby capable of learning anything. Taking this as a starting point, the instructor commits to not setting oneself up as an expert and, in a sense, not teaching.

CLEAN UP

Formative assessment is gathered in the student presentations.

ADDITIONAL RESOURCES

Ranciere, Jacques. *The Ignorant Schoolmaster: Five Lessons in Intellectual Emancipation.* Stanford: Stanford University Press, 1991.

Four Potluck Dishes and a Discovery Tool

Laura Graveline, Visual Arts Librarian, Dartmouth College, laura.graveline@dartmouth.edu

NUTRITION INFORMATION

Students are placed into four groups, and each given a topic or statement to research in any source of their choosing, without specific instructions from the librarian. This gives the students an opportunity to work together, and share ideas and research skills. When each group presents the first set of results, they have an opportunity to discuss why they choose that specific search strategy, and what they think of the results they found. This is also the ideal time for the librarian to suggest other possible search strategies, and demonstrate these strategies with a discovery tool. The librarian and the students can then consider the different results, and students are then given another opportunity to work in their group and try new search strategies utilizing the discovery tool. They can then present their second round of results, and assess the academic relevance of the new results.

Learning Outcomes

Students will be able to:
- Search a discovery tool, applying Boolean logic and utilizing subject headings to refine their search and retrieve articles that are research focused.
- Assess and appreciate the differences between information and articles found searching the internet with a search engine, versus articles found searching with a discovery tool.
- Critically assess the information they retrieve for subject relevance as well as academic criteria, such as determining if articles are peer-reviewed.

NUMBER SERVED

12 to 16 students

COOKING TIME

Prep time: 30 minutes; cooking time: 60 minutes.

DIETARY GUIDELINES

Frame: Searching as Strategic Exploration

Knowledge Practice:
- Students match information needs and search strategies to appropriate search tools.
- Students utilize divergent (e.g., brainstorming) and convergent (e.g., selecting the best source) thinking when searching.

Disposition:
- Students realize that information sources vary greatly in content and format and have varying relevance and value, depending on the needs and nature of the search.

INGREDIENTS & EQUIPMENT

- A flexible classroom so students can sit together in four groups
- Internet access for student computers
- Projector for students and instructor to share

PREPARATION

- The librarian should consult with the instructor to develop four distinct topics or themes for each student group to research.
- I have used this idea with diverse first-year classes looking at such varied ideas as the concept of property in colonial America, hip hop culture, copyright in the visual arts, and Orozco and the Mexican muralists.

COOKING METHOD

1. Students are randomly divided into four groups, and randomly assigned one of four topics.
2. They are given 10 minutes to find as much information as they can about the topic on their own, searching anyway they choose (Google, Wikipedia, library resource, etc.) without any instructions from the librarian. Then each group presents their findings to the class (five minutes for each group).

3. As they present their findings, each group is asked where they found their information, and how they would evaluate the content. It is a chance to discuss and demonstrate the different results found when students try Google vs. a discovery tool.

4. The librarian can take some time to discuss the different databases covered in a discovery tool search that may not be found within an internet search, and why one might want to search a particular library database. It is also an opportunity to discuss what peer-reviewed sources are and why these are important to include in their research.

5. In addition, the librarian can take time to show students how to refine their search using discovery tool facets or advance search options.

6. Often students will find a Wikipedia entry for their topic, via Google, during their first ten minutes of searching. This can lead into a discussion about evaluating internet sources and effective uses of Wikipedia.

7. Students are then given another 10 minutes to research, focusing on a discovery tool and other relevant resources the librarian or instructor may suggest, such as article indexes and research databases the library subscribes to.

8. Students present their findings and discuss if or how it was different in comparison to their original search.

ALLERGY WARNINGS

This approach can feel a bit risky. It is possible to have groups of students immediately go to a discovery tool at the start of the lesson. I have found that allowing students to dive in on their own, and then discuss and sometimes validate what they may have found, seems to make a stronger impression, and definitely has created some lively discussions in class, between students, the instructor, and myself.

CHEF'S NOTES

All of these classes were first-year writing classes or seminars, except for a copyright class, which was an upper-level drawing class. It can be helpful to develop a research guide for each class with helpful search hints or database suggestions that students can refer to after the class.

Reduction Deduction:
Facets as a Key Ingredient to Searching Effectively in a Discovery Layer

Stephanie Graves, Director of Learning and Outreach, Texas A&M University, stephaniegraves@library.tamu.edu; Sarah LeMire, First Year Experience and Outreach Librarian, Texas A&M University, slemire@library.tamu.edu

NUTRITION INFORMATION

One of the benefits of a discovery layer is the large number and variety of results. In order to search effectively, students must learn to narrow down those results in a meaningful way. This activity helps students tap into prior learning by exploring their natural use of facets and limiters in commercial online shopping. Students are then asked to transfer their shopping behaviors into the discovery layer using the facets and limiters.

Learning Outcomes

Students will be able to:

- Apply a facet/limiter to a search in the discovery layer in order to refine search results.
- Describe three facets/limiters that improved their search results in order to know which facets might be beneficial to future searches.

NUMBER SERVED

This recipe can serve as little as two and as many as needed. It scales easily to large and small classes by increasing the size of the groups or doing the activity as individuals.

COOKING TIME

Prep time: 10 minutes
Cooking time: 20 to 30 minutes

DIETARY GUIDELINES

Frame: Searching as Strategic Exploration

Knowledge Practices:

- Design and refine needs and search strategies as necessary, based on search results.
- Understand how information systems (i.e., collections of recorded information) are organized in order to access relevant information.

Dispositions:

- Understand that first attempts at searching do not always produce adequate results.
- Persist in the face of search challenges, and know when they have enough information to complete the information task.

INGREDIENTS & EQUIPMENT

- Internet access
- Student computers
- Activity worksheet

PREPARATION

The librarian will need to identify shopping scenarios and companion websites that would be familiar to the students. The included activity worksheet presents a set of example scenarios and websites.

COOKING METHOD

1. Icebreaker—2 minutes
   a. Ask the students if they like to shop online and what items they shop for. This icebreaker will encourage engagement early in the session.
   b. Explain the goal for the session—students will explore skills that they use to do online shopping which will improve their research skills.
2. Explanation—2 minutes
   a. Explain that commercial shopping websites are like discovery tools. When students are researching, they are shopping for good sources.
   b. Introduce the idea of limiters as a value-added function of discovery tools. Tell students that they already know how to use them in their personal lives.
3. Activity—5 to 7 minutes
   a. Group students into small teams and give them a worksheet (Figure 1).

FIGURE 1. Reduction Deduction Worksheet

SHOPPING EFFECTIVELY USING FACETS

Instructions: Each group will be assigned one of the following scenarios. Using the website provided, try to find the item using the categories and filters of the website. Take notes on what steps you use so that you can report back to the class.

	Shopping Problem	Website	Steps
#1	Your best friend is getting married and you want to buy them some cookware. Find a stainless steel saute pan for under $200.	williams-sonoma.com	
#2	You need shoes for a formal dinner, but you hate high heels and you have less than $50. You are a size 8.5. Find a women's black heeled shoe that is under 2 inches and in your budget.	zappos.com	
#3	You just joined the Football team. You need new cleats. They have to be Nike brand and match your school colors (black and red). Find the best cleats you can for around $100.	champssports.com	
#4	You finished your midterms just in time to realize that Halloween is coming up and you don't have a costume! Find a scary-themed costume in your size that is under $100. Bonus points if the costume is related to food.	Amazon.com	
#5	You want to buy a used car to get to your job as a chef. You've got $8,000 dollars and would really like a Ford truck. Mileage is also important to you. Can you find a truck that you can afford with less than 75,000 miles?	ebay.com	
#6	Your computer died. You need a new laptop fast! Your culinary university offers a discount if you buy an Apple laptop. What is the lowest cost but highest rated laptop that you can get for under $300?	bestbuy.com	
#7	You got an interview for a full-time job, but you don't have anything to wear. Find a black Calvin Klein suit in your size.	macys.com	

SHOP YOUR RESEARCH TOPIC

Instructions: Each individual will apply the limiting techniques from the shopping examples to library searching. Using the library's discovery layer, try to find information sources for your topic. Take notes on which steps you used, and then describe which three steps you found were most helpful for your topic.

Topic:	Steps

Which three facets/limiters improved your search results? Why were they helpful?

b. Explain that groups have to find the item described in their shopping scenario. using the website you have given them and by using the facets and limiters of the site.

c. Remind them to take notes about their process.

d. Assign each group one of the shopping scenarios and websites.

e. Groups compete to see who can find their item fastest using the facets and limiters of their assigned website.

4. Demonstration—5 minutes

a. Ask one to two groups to demo their technique of finding their item, teaching each other about the facets they used to accomplish the task.

5. Transference—10 minutes

a. Have students turn to the back side of their worksheet.

b. Using an example topic, type in keywords in the discovery layer.

c. Explain at least three of the facets/limiters in your discovery layer. Examples include:
   » Date ranges and currency issues
   » Format limiters and types of information
   » Peer-review limiter and issues of authoritativeness

d. Ask students to research their own topic and explore the limiters and facets.

e. Students fill out the back side of worksheet, describing which three limiters/facets improved their search results and why.

ALLERGY WARNINGS

Commercial websites have a tendency to change rapidly. Be sure to check your example websites before class. Be ready to discuss the function of the facets in your discovery layer. Some are apparent to a majority of students; others are more nuanced. If students do not have a research topic prepared, have a few examples that they can use in order to experiment with the facets.

CHEFS' NOTES

Students love this activity because they begin to see the relationship between a natural behavior (shopping) and their assignment (researching). This activity helps with transference, whereby students see the connection between the "real world" and their academic endeavors. Researching becomes less intimidating when couched in terms that they already understand. As a bonus, some students love the idea that they learned how to make their holiday shopping faster and easier.

CLEAN UP

Worksheets are gathered at the end of class to assess the outcomes.

Time-Limited Tapas

Rhiannon Jones, MBA/EMBA Liaison Librarian, University of Calgary, Rc.jones@ucalgary.ca

NUTRITION INFORMATION

This easy-to-prepare group lesson can be planned and executed quickly on short notice. Our lesson times are frequently limited, so it is our responsibility to teach practical, transferable skills. The original lesson plan was aimed at a group of full-time working professionals who expect a high level of service, but also require basic research skills. This recipe can be adapted to any learning level, in any discipline, where time is of the essence.

Learning Outcomes

Students will be able to:

- Be able to use a discovery tool search interface to find known items.
- Use limiters to narrow search results for general research.
- Locate full-text items.

NUMBER SERVED

Best served to smaller classes

COOKING TIME

Prep time: 1 hour
Lesson length: 30 minutes

DIETARY GUIDELINES

Frame: Searching as Strategic Exploration

FIGURE 1. Activity One: Find the Article

Working in small groups, find the following article and answer the questions below. (insert a citation for a class or subject specific known item here)

1. What is the background of the authors?
2. What is the first title in the reference list?
3. Scan the abstract. What is the article about?

Knowledge Practices:

- Match information needs and search strategies to appropriate search tools.
- Use different types of searching language (e.g., controlled vocabulary, keywords, natural language) appropriately.

Dispositions:

- Realize that information sources vary greatly in content and format and have varying relevance and value, depending on the needs and nature of the search.
- Exhibit mental flexibility and creativity.

INGREDIENTS & EQUIPMENT

- Classroom with computers or student devices
- Projector
- Handout for activity one: find the article (Figure 1)
- Handout for activity two: general research (Figure 2)

FIGURE 2. Activity Two: General Research
Your topic is_____. In the same groups, work together to find three resources (books and/or articles). Include titles and one reason why you selected the title.

Title	Reason

PREPARATION

- Locate resources that apply to the class and level for the "find the article" handout. You should choose items that students will need in their coursework.
- Modify the handout, as needed with known items for students to search.
- Make copies of print handouts.

COOKING METHOD

1. This lesson begins with a discussion about the library discovery tool and ends with two group activities with a focus on rapid retrieval.

2. **Warm-up** (3 minutes): Begin by showing the class the library website and talking about various features. Be honest about the strengths and weaknesses of the features. For example, the search interface at the University of Calgary is great for general research, but does not index current business materials.

3. **Known item searching** (5 minutes): Discuss the idea of known item searching by discussing course readings and the availability of e-texts. Do a sample search for one or two of the course readings for the class, preferably by focusing on one easy-to-find item and one difficult item.

4. **Activity one—race to the item** (5 minutes): Wait until now to pass out the handout so students cannot cheat. This may take a little bit longer depending on the size of the group. In small groups, students must find the item and answer the questions correctly on their

handout. The first group to raise their hands and call out the correct answers 'wins.'

5. **Sum-up** (2 minutes): Discuss specific challenges the groups had when locating the known item. Depending on the level of the class, you can choose more difficult material such as book chapters, or you can keep it to a simple full-text article discovery.

6. **General research** (5 minutes): Talk about the challenges of doing research for an assignment, such as breaking down a topic or finding relevant material. Then perform a sample search related to the course and use the results to show limiters and talk about ranking systems.

7. **Activity Two—Top Results** (3 minutes): In same groups, students use the discovery tools to rapidly find three resources for a class assignment or a relevant topic. Under the tight time constraints, they will be forced to look at key aspects of a resource make decisions such as title, abstract, authorship, and source.

8. **Sum-up** (5 minutes): Groups have one minute to showcase their number one result.

9. **Conclusions** (2 minutes): Talk about difficulties with rapid searching. Discuss how research is not a five-minute process, and explain how these tools help them gather enough information to get them started.

ALLERGY WARNINGS

Since this is a lesson plan that is aimed for short sessions, it is important to be aware of the number of students in advance. If possible, it is helpful to reorganize a room prior to class starting. If room configuration is not possible, get the students to form small groups as soon as they enter the class.

CHEF'S NOTE

This is a rapid exercise that should only replace in-depth sessions under time constraints. Students will leave with triage skills that can be built upon once the librarian establishes an academic relationship with the student. Be prepared to watch the time carefully.

CLEAN UP

Formative assessment can be done very informally by noting the pace of the activities and the fulfillment stage when students find the items. Engaged learners will be actively involved in group discussions and the rapid pace of the activities should prevent boredom. This activity can be modified to meet the needs of any subject area, so relevance will be established in the beginning.

Discovery Tool Scavenger Hunt

Laura Nagel, Reference & Instruction Librarian, Clark College, lnagel@clark.edu

NUTRITION INFORMATION

Students have one to two minutes to explore the results of a search in the discovery tool. Each student has a particular question to guide their hunt and gets a chance to quickly show how they found the answer to the whole class.

Learning Outcomes

Students will be able to:
- Find books, articles, or other appropriate resources using the discovery tool.
- Identify discovery tool facets that allow them to narrow or broaden their search.

NUMBER SERVED

10 to 25 students

COOKING TIME

Preparation time: 30 to 45 minutes (for initial question writing and testing)
Length of lesson: 15 to 30 minutes

DIETARY GUIDELINES

Frame: Research as Inquiry

Knowledge Practices:
- Deal with complex research by breaking complex questions into simple ones, limiting the scope of investigations.
- Use various research methods, based on need, circumstance, and type of inquiry.

Dispositions:
- Consider research as open-ended exploration and engagement with information.
- Value intellectual curiosity in developing questions and learning new investigative methods

INGREDIENTS & EQUIPMENT

- A list of questions that will direct the students' scavenger hunt and that they will answer for the whole class (see samples under Additional Resources).
- A wireless mouse or laser pointer that students can pass around to demonstrate with.
- A paper or online survey for assessment

PREPARATION

- Write and test scavenger hunt questions.
- Prepare a sample search topic.
- Contact the instructor to find out how many students will be in the class.
- Write assessment survey prompts.

COOKING METHOD

1. Pass out a scavenger hunt question to each student or have questions at each seat when they arrive.
2. Have all students conduct the sample search in the discovery tool and tell students they will have one to two minutes to hunt around for the answer to their question before showing the answer to the class.
3. Assure them that it's okay if they aren't sure whether their answer is correct or if they can't find it.
4. When you are ready to begin the class activity, give a wireless mouse or laser pointer to the first student.
5. Have the student read their question and demonstrate the answer for the class.
6. Clarify any questions they have or help them find the answer if they were incorrect or couldn't find it.
7. Continue through the group until all questions have been answered. This is meant to be an introduction, so you shouldn't spend too much time on each question unless it seems especially confusing to the students.
8. Finish the activity by asking if anyone has any questions now that the scavenger hunt has been concluded.

ALLERGY WARNING

This activity is especially helpful when students don't have individual topics and just need an overview or introduction to the discovery tool itself.

CHEF'S NOTES

I like this activity because the students are teaching each other by drawing on previous experiences and knowledge.

CLEAN UP

Create a survey where students are given a specific set of qualities and instruct them to find an item that fits those specifications (Figure 1). You may want to come up with two or three different sets of qualities and ask them to find one resource for each.

This assessment allows students to use the knowledge they've just acquired to find an appropriate resource using facets that change their search.

ADDITIONAL RESOURCES

Sample questions:

9. Pick a print book. What is the call number?
10. How do I narrow down to just e-books?
11. How do I narrow down to just articles?
12. How do I change the publication date to the past 10 years?
13. How do I see all of the subjects?
14. How could I narrow down my search?
15. How can I see which books are in the Reference collection?
16. How can I sort the results by publication date?
17. How can I find a citation for an article?
18. How can I e-mail a book's information to myself?
19. How can I search more libraries for this topic?

FIGURE 1. Sample Survey

Scavenger Hunt Follow-Up

Find a print book about college costs that was published in the last 5 years that has a subject term with the word "education" in it. E-mail me the result and write the title and call number below!

Submit

Never submit passwords through Google Forms.

Powered by
Google Forms

This content is neither created nor endorsed by Google.
Report Abuse - Terms of Service - Additional Terms

Document Analysis with Holocaust Era Passports

Brantley Palmer, Assistant Archivist, Keene State College, brantley.palmer@keene.edu; Rodney Obien, Head of Special Collections & Archives, robien@keene.edu, Keene State College

NUTRITION INFORMATION

The students will gain direct experience working with Holocaust studies-related primary sources in collaboration with other students and discuss as a group the importance of the documents. This lesson can be adapted for use with any digitized primary source content that is available through the discovery tool. They will also learn to use a discovery tool and web applications in primary research.

Learning Outcomes

Students will be able to:
- Determine subject, narrative, and research applications of primary sources.
- Demonstrate the interpretative and analytical skills needed to conduct primary source research.

NUMBER SERVED

3 to 30 students

COOKING TIME

Preparation time: 10 to 15 minutes
Cooking time: 45 minutes

DIETARY GUIDELINES:

Frame: Research as Inquiry

Knowledge Practices:
- Use various research methods, based on need, circumstance, and type of inquiry.
- Draw reasonable conclusions based on the analysis and interpretation of information.

Dispositions:
- Value intellectual curiosity in developing questions and learning new investigative methods.
- Value persistence, adaptability, and flexibility and recognize that ambiguity can benefit the research process.

INGREDIENTS & EQUIPMENT

- Computer or mobile device for each student
- Internet access

PREPARATION

- Print out the National Archives' document analysis sheet found at http://www.archives.gov/education/lessons/worksheets/written_document_analysis_worksheet.pdf.
- If needed, set up laptops or desktop computers for students to use.

COOKING METHOD

1. Students are divided into groups of two to three, depending on how many students are in the class (this can also be expanded to groups of four or five for larger class sizes). Groups will be informed that they will be doing investigative work on the Holocaust. Their tasks will be to:
   a. Decipher the document they're examining.
   b. Identify the subject or individuals involved.
   c. Determine a narrative or story based on the clues in the document.
2. To assist in their investigation, each group will be given a document analysis sheet from the National Archives that were printed prior to the start of the exercise with questions to guide them.
3. Students will be instructed to go to the college's discovery tool using their computer or mobile device.
4. The librarian will give a brief demonstration on the tool's basic search features.
5. Students will locate a digital copy of a Holocaust-era passport found using the discovery tool. The librarian will assist each group with their search as needed. Once the groups have located a scanned Holocaust-era passport, they

will examine it and fill out the document analysis sheet. Students can use their smartphones or computers to access any web apps to help them decipher their documents since they may not be written in English.

6. The librarian will be available for any questions, and will circulate amongst the groups to check student progress.

7. Once the groups have had sufficient time to examine the passport and complete the document analysis sheet, the librarian will ask each group to discuss their findings and answer questions about document type, subject or individuals involved, and narrative.

   a. Each group will be asked how they determined their findings and what clues or search methods were used.

   b. The librarian will discuss with the class about what can be learned about the Holocaust and the individual represented through the passports.

   c. The librarian will also discuss the exercise as an example of the difficulties in doing archival research and the investigative skills needed to locate and evaluate primary sources.

ALLERGY WARNINGS

Providing minimal information about the document is helpful when asking students to problem-solve as a means to decipher a primary source.

CHEFS' NOTE

The collaborative nature and group discussion portions are essential in the investigative and discovery process. Students discover and learn from each other as they conduct their investigative research. This lesson can be used with almost any primary source material. If you want to take this lesson a notch further, have students use the discovery tool to locate background and supporting information related to the primary source you are focusing on.

CLEAN UP

The lesson will rely on formative and summative assessments. The librarian will monitor each group to determine their progress and to adjust the exercise or assist students as needed. The document analysis forms will serve as an assessment to determine the effectiveness of each group in deciphering the contents of the passport.

Discovery Tools, Fava Beans, and a Nice Chianti:
Searching the Library's Catalog to Locate Tantalizing Topics within the Collection

Jennifer Pate, Research and Instructional Services Librarian, The University of Alabama, jlrichardson5@ua.edu; Erica England, Research and Instructional Services Librarian, The University of Alabama, eengland@ua.edu

NUTRITION INFORMATION
This instruction recipe is intended to introduce first-semester freshman in Academic Potential courses to the library and its resources. Academic Potential courses at this university are designed to assist students in developing practical study strategies, including motivation, self-assessment, personal responsibility, and time management. Library instruction supports these goals by enabling the student to search for materials independently and gives them multiple points of contact within the library for future research needs.

Learning Outcomes
Students will be able to:
- Navigate the library discovery tool to locate resources such as journal articles and books that are in the library's physical and digital collections.
- Retrieve both electronic and physical materials owned by the library.
- Identify major library services in order to confidently access those services.

NUMBER SERVED
10 to 30 students

COOKING TIME
30 minutes prep time for repeated activity topics
60 minutes prep time for new activity topics
60 to 90 minutes for the lesson

DIETARY GUIDELINES:
Frame: Searching as Strategic Exploration

Knowledge Practices:
- Match information needs and search strategies to appropriate search tools.
- Understand how information systems (i.e., collections of recorded information) are organized in order to access relevant information.

Dispositions:
- Understand that first attempts at searching do not always produce adequate results.
- Seek guidance from experts, such as librarians, researchers, and professionals.

INGREDIENTS & EQUIPMENT
- Computers with access to internet for each student
- Workstation/projector for instructor
- Library Search Exercise worksheets for each student
- Whiteboard and markers
- Prizes (pens, pencils, sunglasses, etc.)

PREPARATION
- Have worksheets in groups of two or three (depending on class size, you will split the students into work groups with no more than three to a group).
- Have prizes ready, including a grand prize and consolation prizes.

COOKING METHOD
1. Students are taken on a brief guided tour of the library, highlighting reference and circulation desks, different resources available, and digital signage used to locate materials on each floor.
2. After returning to the classroom, students are given a live demo of the library's website and are introduced to the new metasearch discovery layer, which quickly searches all facets of the library website. Pitfalls and advantages of using this method are discussed.
3. Each student is given a worksheet with an assigned topic. This is where the students are introduced to new flavors; the chosen topics include cannibalism, cults, polygamy, serial killers, eugenics, and the paranormal. Many first-year students do not realize the library owns such fascinating and diverse material.

4. Again using live demo instruction, students are shown how to search different resources within the discovery tool. Sections include:
   » finding a journal article
   » using limiters to narrow journal choices to scholarly/peer-reviewed, with a concise discussion of the major differences between scholarly and popular sources
   » finding a book
   » using limiters to find a book housed in the library
5. Once the live demo is complete, students grouped together by topic and are asked to use the methods they have been taught to select a book housed within the physical library (Figure 1).
6. While the students are working on choosing a book for their group, the library instructors walk around the classroom, helping any who experience difficulties.
7. Once each group has selected a book, they head out on a race through the stacks to locate it on the shelf as quickly as possible, then bring it back to the classroom. The first group back gets a prize.
8. If some students come back without a book, this is a great opportunity for the librarians to open a discussion with the students about why that may have happened.

ALLERGY WARNINGS

Selecting tantalizing topics, such as cannibalism, cults, and serial killers, engages the

---

FIGURE 1. Library Search Exercise

Name: _____

What's your broad topic? _____

Locate a print book:
Using the discovery tool, find a book related to your topic. To find a book, choose search terms related to your topic, and then click the *Books* limiter on the left-hand side of the screen. When you do a *Books* search, you'll also find E-books. In this case, you'll want to make sure that you find a print book that is available and located in our Library. Limit this by selecting *Catalog Only*. Make sure the record you have chosen has an *Available* status:

Source Types	Limit To
☑ All Results	☐ Full Text
☐ Books (231,743)	☐ Scholarly (Peer Reviewed) Journals
☐ Academic Journals (116,552)	☑ Catalog Only
☐ News (14,946)	
☐ Biographies (11,820)	1978 Publication Date 2013
☐ Magazines (11,381)	
Show More	

⊪ Denying history : who says the **Holocaust** never happened and why do they say it? / Michael Shermer & Alex Grobman , foreword by Arthur Hertzberg.
By: Shermer, Michael. Berkeley, Calif. ; London : University of California Press, c2009. xvii, 334 p. : ill. ; 24 cm. Language: English. Database: University of Alabama Libraries' Classic Catalog
Subjects: **Holocaust denial; Holocaust,** Jewish (1939-1945) -- Historiography
Additional Catalog Information

	Location	Call No.	Status
Book	Gorgas Library	D804.355 .S54 2009	Available

Once you have the call number, you can find the book by checking the digital signage posted between the elevators on every floor of the library. If you're still having difficulties, you can always ask for help at the Information Desk on the first floor or the Circulation Desk on the second floor.

Call #: _____

Author: _____

Title: _____

Please find the print book with your group and bring it back to the classroom!

students and makes them aware that the library's collection contains a wide variety of unusual, offbeat resources.

CHEFS' NOTE
Be prepared for comments from students ranging from, "What is eugenics?" (a great way to introduce discovery options to learn more about your topic before developing keywords), to "These topics are grim". Generally, the students are surprised at the amount of resources they can find on the odd and offbeat subjects.

CLEAN UP
Students are given information about how to access the course LibGuide and how to contact the reference librarians should they need further assistance. We also promote our outreach hours at Student Support Services. You can get a general idea of the success of the lesson by how many students were able to locate a book in the discovery tool, navigate to the correct floor/shelf, and bring the item back to the classroom versus how many struggled with the task. The final section of their worksheet has a fill-in-the-blank Q&A to assess how much information they retained from the tour at the beginning of the session. Some instructors like to have the students turn this entire worksheet in for a grade.

Finding the Right Ingredients:
Using Discovery Layers to Find Different Types of Sources

Lorelei Rutledge, Faculty Services Librarian, University of Utah, Lorelei.Rutledge@utah.edu; Sarah LeMire, First Year Experience and Outreach Librarian, Texas A&M University, slemire@library.tamu.edu

NUTRITION INFORMATION

This recipe was created to encourage first-year students to explore the different flavors of materials available in the library using the discovery layer.

Learning Outcomes

Students will be able to:

- Identify multiple formats of information in print and electronic media in order to understand the types of content delivered by a discovery tool.
- Articulate at least two characteristics of each information format covered.

NUMBER SERVED

20 to 30 students

COOKING TIME

15 to 20 minute activity
20 minutes prep time

DIETARY GUIDELINES

Frame: Information Creation as a Process

Knowledge Practices:

- Articulate the capabilities and constraints of information developed through various creation processes.

- Recognize that information may be perceived differently based on the format in which it is packaged.

Dispositions:

- Are inclined to seek out characteristics of information products that indicate the underlying creation process.
- Value the process of matching an information need with an appropriate product.

INGREDIENTS & EQUIPMENT

- Computer access for all students
- Space to sit in groups of four or five
- A print item for each major format described in the discovery layer (e.g. books, articles, videos).

PREPARATION

- Retrieve an example of each format in print version for students to compare to the format examples found in the discovery layer.
- Create a worksheet (Figure 1) where students can:
  - » List the digital example of each format they find in the discovery layer.
  - » List the print example of each format they identify from the print versions provided.

  - » Fill in their observations about each format.

COOKING METHOD

1. Introduction
   a. Explain how the discovery layer includes resources from different formats and why being able to recognize and understand the characteristics of different formats is important.
2. Activity
   a. Divide students into groups of four or five. Assign each group a format type.
   b. Provide each group a worksheet where they can record a digital example of their format, a print example of each format, and their observations of the characteristics of each format.
   c. First, students will use the discovery layer to search for a topic of interest.
      » Students will use icons and citation information to identify their format (e.g. books).
      » Students will record an example title from the discovery layer for their source format on their worksheet.

FIGURE 1. Characteristics of Different Publications

	Title from discovery layer	Title from provided items	Who writes this type of source? (e.g. scholars, journalists)	Who reads this type of source? (e.g. scholars, general public, students)	What kind of evidence is provided? (e.g. citations, research data)
Journal					
Book					
Review					
Article					
Reference Entry					
Audio or Video					

d. Next, students will record an example title from the print format versions provided for their source format on their worksheet.
e. Finally, students will compare the print and digital examples of their source format and record their observations of characteristics for that format.

3. Discussion
a. Students will share group results with the class, explaining their format's characteristics.
b. Librarian will lead a discussion about what makes each format of information different (e.g. different formats may have different audiences and content types).
c. Explain how recognizing different source formats in the discovery layer can help students identify content that will be best suited for their projects or research.

ALLERGY WARNINGS
Ensure that you have enough copies of each print source format (e.g. bound journals) for each group to have at least one.

CHEF'S NOTES
This activity was created to help students discern the differences between materials such as an e-book and a reference entry. It gives students an opportunity to explore information formats in two different modalities and is intended to help them see different examples of what each format can look like.

CLEAN UP
Don't forget to collect students' worksheets! These artifacts are useful summative assessment tools, and evaluating this work against a rubric can help you determine whether learning objectives are being accomplished.

Research Tool Tasting Menu Accompanied by Anonymous Wombats, Narwhals, and Nyan Cats:
Using Collaborative Google Docs to Create Group Research Activities that Promote Exploration and Collaborative Inquiry

Nancy Schuler, e-Resources & Instructional Services Librarian, Eckerd College, schulenl@eckerd.edu

NUTRITION INFORMATION
The Research Tool Tasting Menu is an interactive group research session where students explore the library's discovery tool and compare it to an e-book collection, specialized database, reference database, and internet search engine. Students complete a shared Google document, where they are identified as anonymous animals. This allows them to see each other's responses which encourages participation and engagement. The activity will enable students to evaluate a discovery tool, consider the pros and cons of different research tools, and determine what tools are best used for different situations.

Learning Outcomes
Students will be able to:
- Utilize basic research skills for finding relevant sources that can be used across multiple research tools.
- Compare different research tools to identify unique features of each.
- Select an appropriate research tool based on their research needs.

NUMBER SERVED
12 to 30 students (divided into 4 to 6 groups, 3–5 members per group)

COOKING TIME
Prep time: 60 minutes
Lesson delivery: 60 to 90 minutes

DIETARY GUIDELINES
Frame 1: Research as Inquiry

Knowledge Practice:
Use various research methods, based on need, circumstance, and type of inquiry.

Disposition:
Seek multiple perspectives during information gathering and assessment.

Frame 2: Searching as Strategic Exploration

Knowledge Practices:
- Utilize divergent (e.g., brainstorming) and convergent (e.g., selecting the best source) thinking when searching.
- Match information needs and search strategies to appropriate search tools.

Disposition:
Realize that information sources vary greatly in content and format and have varying relevance and value, depending on the needs and nature of the search.

INGREDIENTS & EQUIPMENT
- Computer (at least one per group)
- Document sharing tool such as Google Drive document, Microsoft Word Online, Hackpad
- Projector and screen

PREPARATION
- Using the document sharing tool, create a shared document that allows anyone with a link to edit the contents. Create the document in landscape format so that results are more clearly displayed on screen.
- In the document, compile sample research topic ideas for the class to vote on.
- Depending on the research parameters of the class, a "fun" topic could be used (e.g. mating habits of narwhals, comfort food and nostalgia, hashtag activism).

- Write out group instructions on the document.
- Create a table that includes columns for each group and their assigned research tool, including a discovery tool that all groups will search.
- For each row, create questions for groups to answer, such as those listed in the sample *Research Tool Tasting Menu*.

COOKING METHOD

1. Discuss goals of the class, including tie-ins to class assignments related to the library session.

2. Review the four to five research tools to be used in class and where to locate them. Identify special features of each tool (e.g. e-mail articles, citation tools, etc.).

3. Briefly review basic search strategies (e.g. keyword searching, Boolean operators, subject headings).

FIGURE 1. In-class Research Assignment
(Put the link to your shared document here.)

INSTRUCTIONS:
- Break into groups of 3 to 5 people.
- As a group, search _____ (insert the name of your Library's Discovery tool) and the assigned research tool for your group.
  - » You do not need to list the resources you find. Instead, evaluate the results you receive and consider why you received them.
  - » Try to get the best results you can by using various search strategies and special features of the tool you are using.
- Fill in the table below with your findings.
- Be prepared to demo your searches at the end of class.

RESEARCH TOOL TASTING MENU

	ALL Groups *Discovery tool*	**Group 1** *Online reference collection*	**Group 2** *e-book collection*	**Group 3** *Specialized database*	**Group 4** *Google*
What kind of resources does this tool include? (e.g. journals, magazines, websites, etc.)					
What keywords gave you the most successful search results?					
Search strategies used (e.g. phrase searching, AND/OR/NOT, wildcards, etc.)					
Special features used (subject headings, limiters, citation tool, email tool, etc.)					
Pros of this tool					
Cons of this tool					

4. Introduce class research activity. Display shared class research worksheet (Figure 1), including shortened link to shared document. Instruct students to go to shared worksheet on their computers.

5. Have class vote on a single research topic that the entire class will use.

6. Present remaining worksheet and assign groups of students to research the discovery tool plus one additional research tool, and fill in the table with results. Let students know that they will have to present their research results.

7. Research time (10 to 15 minutes): Walk around to assist each group, giving helpful suggestions, and clarifying any questions.

8. Presentation time (20 minutes): Have each group present their findings in three to five minutes. Be sure to highlight any good points made, and mention any important points not addressed.

9. Wrap-up: Ask follow-up questions to summarize activity and re-emphasize original goals of the session. Sample questions:

   » Which tool was hardest/easiest to use?

   » What tool would you use if you were looking for scholarly articles?

   » What tool would you use if you wanted background information?

ALLERGY WARNINGS

Let students briefly experiment with the worksheet to make sure it works for everyone. When including Google as a search tool, be prepared for students to bring up Google Scholar. Be prepared to discuss the basics of evaluating websites.

CHEF'S NOTE

The interactive and shared nature of using a Google document really encourages student participation and creates a positive group experience. Instead of being asked to find specific resources, students are tasked at evaluating search tools as a whole. The follow-up discussion allows students to learn from each other, with reinforcement from the librarian.

CLEAN UP

Use a post-instruction evaluation form to seek student input on the session, including targeted questions on research tools used, as well as overall feedback on the session.

Cooking up Questions:
Using Subject-Specific Online Encyclopedia Articles in the Topic Refinement Process

Christy R. Stevens, Head of Reference and Instruction, Cal Poly Pomona, crs7772@gmail.com

NUTRITION INFORMATION
This in-class group activity was designed for a credit-bearing information literacy class, but it could be used in a one-shot or by any instructor who wants to introduce students to use subject-specific encyclopedias as a means of finding high-quality background information on their topics.

Learning Outcomes
Students will be able to:
- Use the library's discovery tool in order to search specifically for articles in the library's collection of online specialized encyclopedias.
- Use a subject-specific encyclopedia article in order to identify specific issues revolving around their topic.
- Refine their general topic in order to develop a more specific research question.

NUMBER SERVED
Works well with 20 to 30 students broken up into five groups.

COOKING TIME
Prep time: 30 minutes
Cooking time: 45 minutes

DIETARY GUIDELINES
Frame 1: Research as Inquiry

Knowledge Practices:
- Formulate questions for research based on information gaps or on reexamination of existing, possibly conflicting, information.
- Determine an appropriate scope of investigation.

Dispositions:
- Consider research as open-ended exploration and engagement with information.
- Value intellectual curiosity in developing questions and learning new investigative methods.

Frame 2: Searching as Strategic Exploration

Knowledge Practices:
- Match information needs and search strategies to appropriate search tools.
- Understand how information systems (i.e., collections of recorded information) are organized in order to access relevant information.

Dispositions:
- Determine the initial scope of the task required to meet their information needs.
- Match information needs and search strategies to appropriate search tools.

INGREDIENTS & EQUIPMENT
- Projector
- Online word processing space (e.g., Google Drive)
- Instructional space and semi-mobile furniture (chairs that can turn around).
- Computers. If furniture is static, devices like tablets that allow students to move around the room to form groups may be needed.

PREPARATION
- Post directions on a PowerPoint slide or a Google document so they can be projected on the screen in class.
- Select general topics relevant to the theme of the class, and test them to ensure that the library has relevant online specialized encyclopedias.
- Create a Google document containing the general topics. Students will use it to share their research questions.

COOKING METHOD
1. Explain why subject specific encyclopedias can be useful.

2. Demonstrate how to use limiters in the discovery tool to find subject-specific encyclopedia articles.

3. Divide class into groups.

4. Give each group a general topic that is relevant to the theme of the course.

5. Groups search for their general topics and then select the most relevant encyclopedia article to read (Figure 1).

6. After reading the article, groups discuss the specific issues they learned about.

7. As a group, they develop a specific research question related to their assigned topic.

8. The instructor projects a shared shortened link to a Google document that contains a list of the assigned general topics.

9. Groups type their research questions into the Google document under their topic.

10. Group reporters go to the instructor station and demonstrate how they found their article, directing the class's attention to a section in the article that helped them construct a specific research question.

11. The entire class workshops the research question, providing feedback about the question's strengths and weaknesses.

ALLERGY WARNINGS

Using a shared link to an open Google document is a quick and easy way to allow everyone in the class to contribute, but users are also anonymous. As a result, some students may be tempted to vandalize other groups' questions or add humorous (or profane) comments to the document. If you have a rowdy class, consider either using a platform that does not allow for anonymity or have students type out their research questions on a Word document at the instructor's station.

CHEF'S NOTE

Prior to this session, the majority of students will have never used or even heard of subject-specific encyclopedias. This activity thus introduces students to an unfamiliar source type that can help them better understand their topics and narrow to a more specific research question while also acknowledging that many students will be reluctant to come to the library to use the print collection of subject-specific encyclopedias. Students are more likely to see the value of this source type when using a discovery tool that makes it quick and convenient to search for their topics across the library's online encyclopedia collection. Students often express surprise during this activity about how many different encyclopedia titles appear in their search results as

FIGURE 1. Sample Search

well as amusement about some of the encyclopedias' very specific areas of focus, from biological invasions to parapsychology. In addition to learning about the existence of subject-specific encyclopedias, students also find this activity valuable because it introduces them to a new strategy for learning more about a topic in order to refine their research focus and formulate a specific and coherent research question, a task that is difficult if not impossible to do well without some basic background knowledge.

CLEAN UP

Assessment is built into the reporting back and workshopping phases of the activity. As students report back, instructors learn how successful students were in:

- using the library's discovery tool to find a relevant encyclopedia article.
- using an encyclopedia article to refine their topic.
- formulating a research question.

In the workshopping phase, the instructor and the class provide specific point-of-need instructional interventions in the form of feedback on the research questions. The feedback gives students concrete ideas and strategies for attempting to improve research questions going forward. In the context of this IL course, students will continue to practice those strategies in their next assignment, which asks them to develop a research question on an information-related topic of their own choosing.

UNIV 101 Appetizer

Patricia Watkins, Research Librarian/Information Resources Coordinator, Embry-Riddle Aeronautical University, watkinsp1@erau.edu

NUTRITION INFORMATION

First-year students at Embry-Riddle Aeronautical University are required to take a one-credit course, UNIV 101, an introduction to various academic and life services on campus. One segment of UNIV 101 includes a 'one-shot' introduction to the library. This lesson is designed with speed in mind: we are assigned a limited amount of time (anywhere from 20 to 60 minutes) to teach students about library services and resources with the aim of having students up and searching quickly. We may see many of these same students later in the semester in their two-hour library information literacy segment which is imbedded in a required general education communications course where they learn in-depth search strategies. The goal of this "recipe" is to have students quickly learn how to conduct research using the library's discovery tool by selecting keywords.

Learning Outcomes

Students will be able to:

- Use the library discovery tool to retrieve books, e-books or articles with relevance to their degree programs.
- Identify keywords to construct search statements and topic-relevant vocabulary.

NUMBER SERVED

20 to 40 students

COOKING TIME

Cooking time: 20 to 60 minutes
Prep time: 2 hours

DIETARY GUIDELINES

Frame: Searching as Strategic Exploration

Knowledge Practices:

- Use different types of searching language (e.g., controlled vocabulary, keywords, natural language) appropriately.
- Match information needs and search strategies to appropriate search tools.

Dispositions:

- Understand that first attempts at research do not always produce adequate results.
- Realize that information sources vary greatly in content and format and have varying relevance and value depending on the needs and nature of the search.

INGREDIENTS & EQUIPMENT

- In-classroom projector, lectern
- Prepared topics for student groups to use in their search "mission"

PREPARATION

- Contact the course instructors to confirm the amount of time to be allocated to the information literacy instruction and the number of students in the class and determine potential research topics.
- Create sample searches that show students the information results from the discovery tool, book catalog or databases.
- Create search topics, enough for each team of five or six students, based on the research projects they will be engaged in during the semester. There are many ways to create a search "mission" for each team: a different topic for each team, using any search tool of their choosing or the same topic for each team but each team uses a different search tool (e.g., team #1 uses the discovery tool; team #2 uses a specified database; team #3 searches the e-book catalog).

COOKING METHOD

1. After a librarian self-introduction and explanation of the lesson plan, students login to the computer and find the library webpage.
2. Familiarize students with the library website. Introduce students to the

location of the links to subject-specific database appropriate to their fields of study and resource guides.

3. Introduce students to the discovery tool's basic search feature and walk them through finding academic sources using the limiters to narrow to books, e-books or articles. Discuss how Boolean logic helps with keyword creation and relevant search strategy.

4. Introduce elements of CARS (Credibility, Accuracy, Reasonableness and Support) as they relate to searching the web.

5. After the introduction to library resources and search strategies, divide the students into teams of five to six, explaining their "mission" (research topic). Each team will use the library tools they just learned about to search for information related to their given topic. Suggest that they appoint a notetaker to keep track of their search strategies.

6. After about 10 minutes, each team selects a spokesperson to come to the classroom lectern and present to the class the search tool they used, the kind of information discovered and its relation to their topic.

ALLERGY WARNINGS

Sometimes students, shy about coming to the front of the room to navigate their search "mission," can be allowed to share their research from behind their computer in their classroom seat or nominate another spokesperson. Sometimes, I might ask a student to direct me to their search tool as I navigate and they explain what they found. If you run out of time, just pick just one or two teams to share their "mission" findings. At the end of a class, I offer to share key points of the presentation with the faculty so they can post to their course management page for students and offer my contact information to students and faculty for research consultation.

CHEF'S NOTE

We still hear some faculty instruct first-year students to "just Google it" as their main gateway to research. This class is intended as an introduction to novice researchers in the use of the academic discovery tool as an alternative to Google, offering new learners a comparably simple search experience, broadening their search abilities, and introducing them to academic content. If time permits, we provide brief instruction in importance and use of Google Scholar.

CLEAN UP

A post-assessment survey is sent to faculty after the class with a request that faculty ask students to complete it. The survey is a set of six multiple-choice questions plus an open-ended comment section. Data collected include demographics such as class status, the degree or college enrolled in, and the class in which the instruction was delivered. Using a five-point scale, students rate different aspects of the instruction they received for importance, newness, helpfulness and relevance to their research and classes. At the end of the semester, we also send an e-mail to all faculty involved in these sessions to obtain feedback that allows for continuous improvement and changes to the lesson plans in future. Survey results are provided to library management in support of strategic planning initiatives.

4. MEAL PLANS
full lesson plans

Know your Research Game Plan!

Ashley Blinstrub, Research and Assessment Librarian, Saginaw Valley State University, ablinstr@svsu.edu

NUTRITION INFORMATION

In this lesson the instructor will lead a discussion about how to refine a research topic. Students will complete an assignment designed to help them focus on the information they need to find. Students will learn how to craft their searches by using limits to discover narrower topics and learn new lines of inquiry. This activity will also teach them to value persistence, adaptability and recognize that ambiguity can benefit the research process.

Learning Outcomes

Students will be able to:

- Construct searches for online resources in order to find information relevant to their needs.
- Formulate keywords in order to find topic-specific sources.
- Determine the scope of needed information in order to answer their research question.

NUMBER SERVED

10 to 30 students

COOKING TIME

Prep Time: 30 to 45 minutes
Lesson Time: 50 to 75 minutes
Assessment Time: 1 to 3 hours

FIGURE 1. Research Game Plan

Your topic:

Break down the concepts within your topic:
(Tip: Keep it simple: one word or phrase per concept).

	AND		AND	

Brainstorm synonyms, alternate spellings, and related topics for each concept:

What KIND of information you need to find?

	Background information
	Historical information
	Biographical information
	Statistics
	Financial information
	Opinions
	Current events
	Opposing Viewpoints
	Research results
	Other?

Where have you already looked for information?

DIETARY GUIDELINES
Frame: Research as Inquiry.

Knowledge Practices:
- Determine an appropriate scope of investigation.
- Deal with complex research by breaking complex questions into simple ones, limiting the scope of investigations.

Dispositions:
- Consider research as open-ended exploration and engagement with information.
- Appreciate that a question may appear to be simple but still disruptive and important to research.

INGREDIENTS & EQUIPMENT
- Research Game Plan (Figure 1)
- Keywords and filters activity (Figure 2)
- Computers with access to internet
- Assessing search results tutorial

PREPARATION
Print the activities, upload them to a website, or e-mail them to the class. It may be helpful to coordinate this with the instructor ahead of time.

COOKING METHOD
1. Give a brief introduction to the library. Explain where the student can get help, where to find library hours and then briefly describe how to navigate the website.

FIGURE 2. Keywords and Filtering

	Search Terms	Filters	# of results	Are the results relevant? Y/N
1		none		
2		Peer-reviewed journals		
3	_____ AND _____	Peer-reviewed journals, Subject: _____		
4	_____ AND _____	Peer-reviewed journals, Subject: _____ Year: 2009-2014		

Explain why the relevancy of results and the number of results changed as you added more filters and keywords to your search.

2. Explain the importance of planning research by narrowing topics, picking out key concepts, brainstorming keywords and knowing what kinds of information they need to find.
3. Introduce the Research Game Plan and then give them time to fill out the sheet for their topics.
4. Explain what a discovery layer is and emphasize that it is a good first stop for research.
5. Demonstrate how to combine different search terms, explaining that it is important to be specific when using a discovery layer.
6. Demonstrate the Research Game Plan to search the discovery layer and point out the filters and what each one does. Explain the purpose of the various filters,

such as scholarly journals, date, subject, etc.
7. After the demonstration, the librarian will prompt the students to use the Research Game Plan that they've filled out to complete the keywords and filters handout.
8. Once that activity is complete, the librarian will engage students in a discussion of how filters and additional keywords narrow and focus search results.
9. Collect the Research Game Plan and keyword activity.
10. After class, scan the return the Research Game Plan and keyword activities to the instructor to distribute to students. You can also collect these via e-mail. (See Clean Up for next steps.)

ALLERGY WARNINGS

Students should have had time to think about their topics and how to narrow them down before the library instruction session. The librarian should discuss with instructor before the session whether the students have topics picked out or not. The instructor should have explained the research assignment to the class prior to the library instruction session.

CHEF'S NOTES

Students sometimes have difficulty determining the main concepts of their research topic. This exercise helps students narrow or broaden their topics and think about the type of sources they may need they start the research process.

CLEAN UP

Librarians will collect completed copies of the Research Game Plan and the keywords activity at the end of the session. Librarians will then scan or copy the activities and send them back to the instructor to distribute to students so students can refer to the worksheets in their research. Once the librarian has collected the scans for the entire class, they will then choose at random 25 percent of the activities to apply to the rubrics (Figures 3 and 4). The

FIGURE 3. Research Game Plan Rubric

	Excellent (4)	Acceptable (3)	Improving (2)	Needs Improvement (1)
Defines Research Question/ Thesis	Defines the research question/thesis in a way that fits the scope of the assignment	Defines the research question/thesis, but the scope is too broad or too narrow	Defines a topic, but now a clear research question/thesis	Does not define a research question/thesis or topic
Scope of the Information Needed	Determines key concepts that reflect the research question/thesis using synonyms and related terms	Determines key concepts that reflect the research question/thesis, but does not identify synonyms and related terms	Determines concepts, using the only the terms included in the research question/thesis	Does not determine any concepts that describe the research question/thesis
Identifies Relevant Types of Information	Identifies subject-relevant information source types appropriate to the research need	Identifies subject-relevant information source types, but the source types are not appropriate to the research need/assignment	Identifies information source types that do not meet the criteria of the research need	Does not identify information source types
Brainstorms Keywords	Brainstorms keywords and synonyms that describe the research question/thesis	Brainstorms keywords that describe the research question/thesis but does not use synonymous terms	Brainstorms inappropriate or misspelled keywords	Does not show evidence of brainstorming keywords

FIGURE 4. Rubric for Filters Activity

	Excellent (4)	Acceptable (3)	Improving (2)	Needs Improvement (1)
Refines Search Using Features	Refines the search as needed using relevant databases limiting features to retrieve results appropriate to the information need	Refines the search as needed using relevant limiting features, but the results are still too broad or too narrow	Refines the search but does not use relevant limiting features	Does not refine the search
Understands why to use different search strategies and filters	Can articulately explain why the relevancy and number of results changes as they use filters and thoughtful search strategies	Can explain why the relevancy or number of results changes as they use filters and search strategies	Can explain why the number of results change as they use filters or search strategies	Cannot explain why the number of results change as they use filters or search strategies

rubrics will assess student knowledge of the learning outcomes. As this assessment will take place outside of the library instruction session, the librarian may have to follow up with the class through another class visit, a research guide or a tutorial in order to reinforce concepts that students struggled with based on their scores. The time these assessments take varies based on the number of students in the class and the percentage of worksheets chosen to assess, but can take anywhere from one to three hours of assessment time.

One Shot at Discovering Library Resources

Ruth M. Castillo, Head of Reference and Instruction, Charleston Southern University, rcastillo@csuniv.edu

NUTRITION INFORMATION

This one-shot instruction session is intended to address a research assignment for lower-division undergraduates. Students work in pairs to develop a research strategy and use a discovery tool to locate information resources.

Learning Outcomes

Students will be able to:

- Construct a search string using relevant keywords and Boolean logic in order to use a discovery tool to retrieve appropriate library resources.
- Recognize the elements of a database entry page in order to evaluate and select relevant resources, and to create a list of the necessary elements needed for citing their selected resources.

NUMBER SERVED

8 to 30 lower-division undergraduate students

COOKING TIME

Prep time: usually less than 30 minutes
Lesson delivery: approximately one hour. It can easily be adapted for 50-minute and 80-minute class periods.

DIETARY GUIDELINES

Frame: Searching as Strategic Exploration

Knowledge Practices:

- Design and refine need and search strategies as necessary, based on search results.
- Manage searching process and results effectively.

Dispositions:

- Understand that first attempts at searching do not always produce adequate results
- Realize that information sources vary greatly in content and format and have varying relevance and value, depending on the needs and nature of the search.

INGREDIENTS & EQUIPMENT

- Copies of worksheet
- Classroom set of computers with a link to the assessment survey
- The instructor's research assignment for the class
- A sample topic that meets the class assignment requirements and offers good results in the discovery tool

PREPARATION

- Make copies of worksheet for the class.
- Review the instructor's assignment.
- Choose a sample topic that works well for the assignment and the discovery tool.

COOKING METHOD

1. Welcome students to the classroom. Have them sit in pairs and pass out worksheets (Figure 1). Instruct students to retrieve their assignment instructions and a pencil.
2. Review the specifics of the assignment with the students and emphasize the requirements for sources allowed by the instructor.
3. Walk students through the process of brainstorming keywords relevant to their topic. In pairs, have students describe their topics to their partners, then write their topics on their worksheets. Typically each student has their own topic, so each pair is working on two topics at the same time.
4. Review what keywords are and what they're used for.
5. Have students work in pairs to create lists of keywords of for each of their topics using the worksheet.
6. Show students how to access the library's discovery tool and demonstrate searching a single keyword. Instruct students to search one of their keywords.

FIGURE 1. Worksheet Sample
Library Resources Guide

Name:_____ Date:_____

Write a short summary of your research topic or question:

List six to eight keywords that apply to your topic: _____

_____

Note which database or search tool you are using today: _____

Write down three searches you plan to try using the Boolean operator 'AND':

Search: _____ AND _____

Search: _____ AND _____

Search: _____ AND _____

For the first resource you choose to e-mail to yourself, write out the information needed to create a citation below:

Article Title:_____

Article Author(s):_____

Journal (Source) Title:_____

Date Published:_____ Volume:_____ Issue:_____ Pages:_____

Format: _____ Database: _____

Remember to e-mail all of the resources you plan to use to yourself.

Number of articles e-mailed today:_____

7. Use the search results to review the following types of sources and their uses:
   a. Reference articles
   b. Books
   c. News articles (periodicals)
   d. Journal articles (academic/scholarly/peer-reviewed)
   e. Book reviews
   f. Other resources
8. Introduce the Boolean operator 'AND', then demonstrate a search string using 'AND'. Have students write three search strings using 'AND' they plan to try on their worksheet.
9. Using the new search results, select one result and use it to explain the following:
   a. How to retrieve full-text
   b. How to identify the parts of the database entry needed for a citation
   c. How to e-mail articles
10. Have students find resources for their assignment and complete worksheet. Instruct students to e-mail their chosen resources to themselves. For one of their resources, have students write out the information needed to create a citation on their worksheet.
11. At the end of the session, have students complete the assessment survey.

ALLERGY WARNINGS

Occasionally a class comes in that has not been given a research assignment. Use generic assignment guidelines and a topic to work through together in this case.

CHEF'S NOTE

I use the following story during the beginning of the session to explain the differences between using Google, a discovery tool, and a subject specific database:

Before we jump into our research today, let's talk about our choices for research tools: Google, a discovery tool, or a subject-specific database. To explain the difference between these three, let's say that doing research is like shopping for chocolate. Every year for my grandfather's birthday we give him chocolate. Now, I could run into a big box store and buy a run-of-the-mill chocolate bar. Not great, but it counts. The problem is, I will probably wander through hundreds of thousands of items in the store, buy plenty of things I don't need, and walk out without remembering to get the chocolate bar. This is like going to Google for a research paper. Sure, you can find information on your topic, but you're not likely to find the best information, and you spend a lot of time wandering around trying to find what you can get.

I could also go to a grocery store. There will be a whole aisle for candy and whole section full of different kinds of chocolate. This is like using a discovery tool. We know that it is full of good information for research, and we can limit our search to the types of resources we need. This is what we are going to do in class today.

Now, sometimes I might want to do something really special like get Grandpa something from the French chocolatier downtown. This is like an in-depth research project that needs the tools and resources of a subject-specific database. We won't get that far today, but if you ever cannot find information that you need for a project, remember to talk to a librarian.

CLEAN UP

This session is assessed with a formal web survey, which is linked from an icon on the desktops of the classroom computers. The survey includes the library's standard instructor evaluation questions followed by open-ended questions to evaluate student understanding and participation in the session.

Word Cloud Search Sushi

Kiersten Cox, Instructor, University of South Florida, cox@usf.edu; James E. Scholz, Graduate Assistant, School of Information, University of South Florida, jscholz@mail.usf.edu

NUTRITION INFORMATION

A seasoned cook understands that not all kitchens are equal; they treat the same ingredients differently, so alternate approaches are required to get best results. With that knowledge in mind, as our aspiring chefs create Word Cloud Sushi, they will do so practicing different types of searching language. For instance, some "dishes" are prepared with a natural language query, some by way of controlled vocabulary, and yet others by way of Boolean logic. Great meals don't just happen; they are the result of a cook's creativity and mental flexibility. Before he or she presents the perfect meal, they present a few duds. That is to be expected, and when they do create just the right dish, those first attempts at searching will have been worth the struggle. We believe that by starting the process in such a creative way as generating word clouds, the "cooking" process starts from a place that is as much play as it is work.

This sushi simplifies identifying keywords and using them when searching with your libraries discovery tool. With its reliance on a visual representation of the important words about a topic, it is the perfect accompaniment to a main course of discovery layer, advanced catalog or database searching.

This lesson has been used as part of an information literacy for-credit course. It is used to introduce the concept of keywords in conjunction with teaching students how to search a university library's discovery layer. We then apply the concepts learned in this lesson to searching databases and web search engines.

Learning Outcomes

Students will be able to:

- Identify words which uniquely identify their research need in the word cloud they create.
- Construct a search statement using the identified keywords in order to search the library catalog.
- Analyze their search results and strategize ways to reformulate the search statement to improve accuracy.

NUMBER SERVED

25 to 30 (but easily able to expand to a larger group)

COOKING TIME

Prep time varies based on knowledge of subject matter. For a subject you know well, allow one hour to develop a good word cloud and to practice using keywords from the cloud. If it is a subject that you are unfamiliar with or if you have never before used a word cloud generator, allow for two hours prep time to become familiar with the ins and outs of the word cloud generator and to practice searching with words from the cloud.

Additionally, allow for an hour of in-class time with students. Spend 10 minutes discussing keywords and keyword searching in the discovery layer, five minutes to demonstrate how to use a word cloud generator, and five minutes demonstrating searching with keywords from the word cloud. Briefly explain the assignment and then allow the rest of the hour for students to create their own cloud and use keywords to search the discovery layer.

DIETARY GUIDELINES

Frame: Searching as Strategic Exploration

Knowledge Practices:

- Design and refine needs and search strategies as necessary based on search results
- Use different types of searching language (e.g., controlled vocabulary, keywords, natural language) appropriately.

Dispositions:

- Exhibit mental flexibility and creativity.
- Understand that first attempts at

searching do not always produce adequate results.

INGREDIENTS & EQUIPMENT
- Computer with projection capabilities and access to the internet
- Students computers with internet access
- Links to several word cloud generators
- Links to several blog sites
- Pre-selected research topics/assignments
- Links to several sources from which students can draw basic information for their word clouds. Examples are Wikipedia, an electronic version of the course textbook, or Tumblr.

PREPARATION
Prepare a demonstration of the process from beginning to end, include a research query, the source for the word cloud, a pre-generated word cloud, examples of search queries using keywords from the cloud, and examples of blog sites.

COOKING METHOD
1. Discuss what the keywords are and demonstrate keyword searching.
2. Describe a pre-selected research need to the students.
3. Ask students to select keywords and demonstrate searching the library discovery layer with a couple of the keywords.
4. Briefly discuss results and mention that some keywords will yield better search results than others because some will be more specific to the topic than others.
5. Go to a previously tested word cloud generator and discuss briefly how it works.
6. Copy and paste either an entire article, relevant portions of text or URL into a word cloud to generate a word cloud for the research topic (Figure 1).
7. Ask students to select keywords from the cloud and demonstrate searching with those keywords.
8. Discuss results and compare them to previous results.
9. Provide links to keyword generator and basic sources such as Wikipedia, or sources specific to the assignment.
10. Have students generate word clouds for their topic by using text or a URL from sources provided in step 8.
11. Have students search the discovery layer using keywords from the word cloud they generated.
12. Ask students to analyze their word cloud and the search results that were produced from the word cloud key words.
13. Wrap up the sushi in a class blog: Students will discuss which of their keyword combinations produced the most helpful results, what sorts of materials they found, what did not work, and why certain keyword combinations worked while others did not.

FIGURE 1. Sample Word Cloud

ALLERGY WARNING

All word cloud generators do not cook up the same results. Test them to learn how they work and how they interact with the learning platform you are using.

Students are sometimes reluctant to choose the best ingredients (keywords). They may want to pick words that are ubiquitous such as adjectives that are descriptive instead of words that would truly focus their search. If time allows have students demonstrate their searches to the class and then discuss what could have been better key terms.

Steps 6 to 13 can be time consuming. You may want to have students do some of the work in class and then finish it up as homework. Having a discussion board or blog for this assignment is very helpful and allows you to track student work done on their own.

CHEF'S NOTE

We've taught this lesson several times and always get good reviews on the classroom blog they are required to post to. One student wrote, "Having to make the word cloud helped me to see distinct keywords throughout these two web pages." The word clouds generate student's excitement for their topics, a key ingredient for Word Cloud Sushi. Searching tends to bring students down a bit. They can be easily frustrated and distracted so it is useful to keep refocusing them by having volunteers show their searches to the class and to have a discussion with them about what they found and how the searches can be tweaked. This can be done while the rest of the class is still working. Watching others flounder and recover is beneficial for them. It reassures them when they don't get it "right" on the first try.

CLEAN UP

In a follow-up class the authors assess student search skills with a scavenger hunt through the discovery layer and databases. Even armed with the knowledge of keywords, students average 78% correct answers. At time of publication we don't have pre-test information, but students self-report that they believe their search skills have increased since completing the word cloud assignment. After the scavenger hunt we discuss the most often missed questions and strategize ways students could have gotten better results.

Finding and Evaluating Sources:
Ingredients for Discovery Tool Success

William Cuthbertson, Instruction Librarian and Assistant Professor, University of Northern Colorado, william.cuthbertson@unco.edu; Stephanie Evers, Instruction Librarian and Lecturer, University of Northern Colorado, stephanie.evers@unco.edu; Brianne Markowski, Instruction Librarian and Assistant Professor, University of Northern Colorado, brianne.markowski@unco.edu

NUTRITION INFORMATION

This library session is served up to students through the English department's first-year writing programing as they are writing their first college research paper. Using small group discussion and an online worksheet guiding students through the research process, this session is designed to introduce students to identifying and evaluating scholarly sources found through our library's discovery tool.

Learning Outcomes

Students will be able to:

- Evaluate abstracts in order to determine if a source is relevant to a research topic.
- Use contextual clues in order to determine if a source is scholarly.
- Discuss the importance of using a bibliography during the research process in order to find additional sources relevant to a research topic.

NUMBER SERVED

This recipe is scalable to the number of computers available to students, but works best with no more than 30 students.

COOKING TIME

Preparation time: Approximately 3 hours. We prepare everything for this lesson at the beginning of the semester and then use the materials throughout the semester.
Lesson delivery: 50-to-75-minutes

DIETARY GUIDELINES

Frame: Authority as Constructed and Contextual

Knowledge Practices:
Use research tools and indicators of authority to determine the credibility of sources, understanding the elements that might temper this credibility.

Disposition:
Motivate themselves to find authoritative sources, recognizing that authority may be conferred or manifested in unexpected ways.

INGREDIENTS & EQUIPMENT

- Computer access for all students
- Three abstracts for evaluation; we suggest two scholarly (one on topic, one very closely related to the topic) and one other article related to the topic

from a publication like *The New Yorker* or *The Atlantic* (use the article's front page rather than abstract, if necessary).
- Evaluation Investigation half-sheets
- Online research worksheet (Google Forms and Qualtrics work well). See Additional Resources for an example.

PREPARATION

- Choose a research topic.
- Find relevant articles for evaluation activity.
- Make copies of abstracts and Evaluation Investigation half-sheets.
- Create the online worksheet and set it up to e-mail students a copy of their responses.

COOKING METHOD

1. Introduction, include learning objectives.
2. Divide class into groups of three. Give each student in the group the Evaluation Investigation half-sheet (Figure 1) and one of the three article abstracts, so that each person in the group is reading a different source. Students work independently to evaluate their abstract using the criteria provided on the half-sheet.

FIGURE 1. Evaluation Investigation
Answer the following individually, for your abstract:

1. Is the abstract for a scholarly journal article? ❏ YES ❏ NO

2. Would you consider the author an expert? ❏ YES ❏ NO
    Why?

3. Would you consider this article timely? ❏ YES ❏ NO

Answer this question together as a group:
1. Which article(s) would your group use for a research paper on the topic, "How does using social media impact loneliness?"

CLEAN UP

Using the online worksheet to record student responses in a spreadsheet allows librarians to gather a large amount of data on how well students meet specific learning objectives.

ADDITIONAL RESOURCES

Online research worksheet example: http://goo.gl/forms/2TGzUzRduM.

3. Then, as a group, students discuss the question, "Which article(s) would you use for a research paper if the topic was, _____?" After small group discussions, ask groups to share their reasoning for selecting the article(s) they chose.

4. Conclude with a quick discussion on how to evaluate a book using the index and table of contents.

5. The instructor demonstrates the discovery tool briefly to remind students about using peer-review limiters, locating article abstracts, and interpreting call number information.

6. For the remainder of the session, students use the discovery tool to conduct research on their own while completing the online research worksheet. This worksheet guides students through the research process by directing them to: come up with topic keywords, find a peer-reviewed article and evaluate it, find a book and evaluate it, and finally, use the bibliography of the article they found to identify and search for an additional source relevant to their topic.

7. The last section of the online worksheet is a formative assessment to be completed in the final minutes of the session.

ALLERGY WARNINGS

This session works best when students can work on their own research for a class assignment. If students don't yet have research topics, distribute suggested topics for them to practice with.

CHEFS' NOTE

Students seem to enjoy filling in an online worksheet and appear much more motivated to finish it compared to paper worksheets used in previous sessions. Students also appreciate that the form is e-mailed to them upon completion so that they have a copy of the work they accomplished in class.

Interactive Discovery:
Puzzling Out Discovery Tool Essentials

William Cuthbertson, Instruction Librarian and Assistant Professor, University of Northern Colorado, william.cuthbertson@unco. edu; Stephanie Evers, Instruction Librarian and Lecturer, University of Northern Colorado, stephanie.evers@unco.edu; Brianne Markowski, Instruction Librarian and Assistant Professor, University of Northern Colorado, brianne.markowski@unco.edu

NUTRITION INFORMATION

This library session is served up to students through the English department's first-year writing program when students are first introduced to the expectations of college-level research. Using a bibliographic puzzle activity and a semi-competitive searching exercise, this session is designed to introduce students to a discovery tool and prepares them to locate the information that they will need to format citations.

Learning Outcomes

Students will be able to:

- Search a discovery tool by a variety of fields in order to find books and articles.
- Interpret a call number in order to locate materials within the library.
- Determine appropriate keywords in order to effectively find sources on a research topic.

NUMBER SERVED

This recipe is scalable to the number of computers available to students, but works best with approximately 24 to 30 students.

COOKING TIME

Prep time: Approximately 2 hours for copy-ing, cutting, and assembling the puzzle packets, results sheets, and worksheets. Cooking time: Best served in a 50-minute classroom session.

DIETARY GUIDELINES

Frame: Searching as Strategic Exploration

Knowledge Practice:
Design and refine needs and search strategies as necessary, based on search results.

Disposition:
Understand that first attempts at searching do not always produce adequate results.

INGREDIENTS & EQUIPMENT

- Computer access for all students
- Prepared puzzle packets (pieces for packets A and B collected in separate manila envelopes with puzzle guides affixed to the outsides of each packet)
- Discovery tool worksheet (two-sided)

PREPARATION

- Assemble puzzle packet A (Figure 1). Copy and cut apart the puzzle pieces which include key parts of one book re-cord (authors, titles, call numbers, etc.)

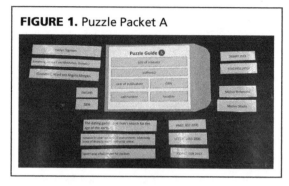
FIGURE 1. Puzzle Packet A

and several additional "false leads". We recommend copying puzzle pieces on cardstock, or having the pieces lami-nated for frequent use.

- Place the puzzle pieces in a manila envelope and affix a puzzle guide to the front of the envelope. The puzzle guide provides students an outline or template of the bibliographic record.
- Repeat for puzzle packet B (Figure 2) which includes a journal article record.

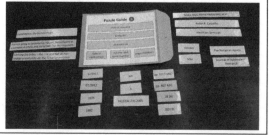
FIGURE 2. Puzzle Packet B

- Photocopy the Discovery Tool Show-down worksheet.
- Each pair of students will receive 1 puzzle packet A, 1 puzzle packet B, and 2 copies of the Discovery Tool Show-down worksheet.

COOKING METHOD

1. Introduction, including explanation of learning objectives.
2. For the first activity, hand pairs of students puzzle packet A. Ask students to empty the packet components onto their table and explain to them that each packet contains pieces (authors, titles, call numbers, etc.) that complete one bibliographic record they will find in the discovery tool. There is only one correct bibliographic record for the students to find in the discovery tool. The packets also contain "false leads"—additional components that they may be able to find in the discovery tool but that won't have all the necessary pieces to match up correctly on the puzzle guide.
3. Students will decide which pieces or fields produce more effective results by using the discovery tool to search for the titles, authors, ISBNs, etc. in their puzzle packets. Once students have located the bibliographic record that solves the puzzle, they will be able to use the information from the discovery tool to match their puzzle pieces to the puzzle guide (title to title, author to author, etc.)
4. When students finish puzzle A, walk around the room to check that they have the correct solution. Prompt students to answer the questions on the Discovery Tool worksheet, part 1 about call numbers and library locations, and hand them puzzle packet B to get started on.
5. After students complete puzzle B, check their solutions and prompt them to answer the questions on the worksheet about article and journal title identification.
6. When all groups have solved the puzzles, transition to the next activity (see the Discovery Tool Showdown, Figure 3). Students work individually on their computers through a guided activity to see who can get the fewest number of relevant search results. The instructor provides the initial keywords or research question, like "How does television advertising affect childhood obesity?"
7. Students search the keywords in the discovery tool and record the number of their results on the Discovery Tool worksheet. With the instructor's guidance, students add limiters (filtering first by journal article, for example, and then, after a short discussion on its definition, by scholarly and peer-review articles). Students then pick an additional keyword to add to the search string, brainstorming with the instructor about possible synonyms. Students continue to record the number of search results after each limiter is applied.
8. Finally, the instructor briefly demonstrates limiting by publication date and by subject before asking students to pick one final limiter and record their number of results. The activity concludes with a conversation about how students came to their final number of results. Prizes can be awarded for the best set of relevant search results, lowest overall number, or best use of limiters.
9. Students use the remainder of the session (10 minutes or so) to search in the discovery tool for sources on a topic either provided by the instructor or for a class assignment and record those findings on the last section of the worksheet. The instructor is available to answer questions one-on-one during this time.
10. In the final minutes of class, students fill out a brief formative assessment.

ALLERGY WARNINGS

Students will usually need extra guidance when first beginning the puzzle activity. The instructor should walk around to the various groups, talking to students about the connections between their search results, the puzzle components, and identifying effective strategies on searching and reading the records in the discovery tool. Students will complete the second puzzle more quickly as they understand searching better and are familiar with the bibliographic components.

CHEF'S NOTE

Students enjoy the puzzle activity and comments such as, "This is actually kind of fun," are sometimes overheard.

CLEAN UP

We ask two questions on our formative assessment:

1. What is one thing from today's session that you still have questions about?
2. What were the two most important things you learned during today's session?

FIGURE 3.

Part 2: Discovery Tool Showdown

Your Keywords (Remember to search phrases by placing them within quotation marks)

Number of Results retrieved based on ONLY your Keywords

Filter #1: _____

Number of Results

Filter #2: _____

Number of Results

(Add an additional keyword)

Number of Results

Filter #3: _____

Number of Results

Use the topic and keywords from above, or your own research topic and find the following:

Use a search string to find a **Scholarly & Peer Reviewed** journal article in the discovery tool about your topic.

Article Title	
Journal or Publication Title	
Volume/Issue	

Use a search string to find a **Book** in the discovery tool about your topic.

Title	
Call Number	

Library Quest:
Hosting a Banquet Feast

Caleb Domsy, Business and eLearning Librarian, Humber College, caleb.domsy@humber.ca; Aliya Dalfen, Liberal Arts & Science, Hospitality, Recreation & Tourism and Student Engagement Librarian, Humber College, aliya.dalfen@humber.ca

NUTRITION INFORMATION

This recipe is designed for large classes, and splits the quest into three distinct challenge areas: physical library space, online research resources, and library services and support. The quest moves groups through the challenge areas at different times, so that only one-third of the class is in the physical library at any given time. By the end of the quest, all teams will have visited the library, researched library resources using a discovery layer, and learned about library services and support. To meet the immediate needs of more complicated tasks within the quest, students are given links to instructional videos. Students also are encouraged to be active in library social media spaces, with book "selfies," and more.

Teams are given an activity sheet with questions to answer and topics to research. Students use their mobile devices (laptops, tablets, or smartphones) to access the library's website and discovery layer for help answering questions. Students are encouraged to use how-to video links included in the activity sheets to support independent learning during the quest. Challenges include finding books in the library and taking "selfies" in the stacks, searching for articles on a topic in the discovery layer, learning citation rules, booking study spaces, and more. In a one-shot library instructional session, the Library Quest has enough information for even the hungriest appetites.

Learning Outcomes
Students will be able to:
- Identify library services and support.
- Locate on-campus and online library resources.
- Perform basic searches using the library's discovery layer.

NUMBER SERVED
This meal can feed small and large classes: anywhere from 30 to 120-plus students.

COOKING TIME
Initial prep for this banquet feast can take time, depending on length, questions and field testing. Give yourself at least a day to create, prep and test your first quest. Optimal cooking time is 75 minutes, but can be completed in a 50-minute time period.

DIETARY GUIDELINES
Frame: Searching as Strategic Exploration

Knowledge Practices:
- Manage searching processes and results effectively.
- Match information needs and search strategies to appropriate search tools.

Dispositions:
- Recognize the value of browsing and other serendipitous methods of information gathering.
- Persist in the face of search challenges, and know when they have enough information to complete the information task.

INGREDIENTS & EQUIPMENT
- At least one smartphone, tablet or laptop per team. *Note:* If the library does not have them to supply, ask students to bring their own mobile device to class.
- Library Quest activity sheets (Figure 1) divided into three different sequences
- Reliable wifi
- Two (or more) librarians or support staff, familiar with teaching and the quest

FIGURE 1. Library Quest Activity Sheet

Sequence 1	Sequence 2	Sequence 3
Discovery layer demonstration *in-class*	Discovery layer demonstration *in-class*	Discovery layer demonstration *in-class*
❑	❑	❑
Services and support *online*	The physical library *in-library*	Research and citation *online*
❑	❑	❑
Research and citation *online*	Services and support *online*	The physical library *in-library*
❑	❑	❑
The physical library *in-library*	Research and citation *online*	Services and supports *online*

PREPARATION

- For the Library Quest to work successfully, you will need a healthy dose of faculty support, as hands-on group activities involving 100+ students are inherently challenging to organize and manage on your own.
- Before the event, we encourage faculty to integrate student credit or reward upon completion of the Library Quest. In the past, faculty credit or reward has varied. Some examples include: prizes, attendance points or a 2 percent grade increase upon completion. In our experience, we have found students will not be as engaged or fully complete the quest without this kind of faculty encouragement.
- In an effort to save time during the day of the event, we request that faculty have their students split into groups of 2 to 3 prior to the quest. In the past, faculty have used their learning management system and class lists to do this. If faculty are not agreeable to this, you can request the class lists in advance, split the groups up on your own, and have the students split up into their designated teams the day of the event. In our experience, the classes where the faculty have organized groups the week prior have worked best. We also ask faculty to remind students to bring their smartphones, tablets, or laptops to class, charged, a week prior to the quest.

- Design Library Quest activity sheets and divide into three different sequences. You may want to include existing or new instructional videos to add a multimedia dimension to the quest. Links to videos can be used as a supplement to instruction and can be accessed on their device. Use different colors and/or numbering systems so that the different versions are not easily confused.

- A few days before the event, send a notice to library staff about the quest so they know to expect a large group of students participating in the activity.
- Print out Library Quest activity sheets. There will be three differently arranged activity sheets that all contain the same questions but in a different order. These are the main instructions the students will be following.
- For the in-library piece of the activity sheet, create any clue sheets required to help facilitate the quest. For example, our library quest asks students to visit each service point (Circulation Desk, Reference Desk and Media Desk), find the clue sheet, and answer a question. The clue sheet will include the information required for students to answer the question correctly. The clue sheets help minimize questions directed at staff and decrease congestion at service points during the quest.

COOKING METHOD

1. Class Introduction: Have students sit in their groups. Describe the rules of the quest: respect library decorum, emphasize team-work, and introduce who to go for help during the quest.
2. Explain how the quest works, with the activity sheet as your guideline. Emphasize that groups must complete the activity sheet in the given order. You may want to do a quick demonstration

of your discovery layer beforehand (no more than 3 to 5 minutes). Give students a deadline for them to hand in the activity sheet.

3. Hand out the Library Quest activity sheets. Three versions should be distributed evenly among the teams. Students will now begin the quest.

4. Students will follow the Library Quest activity sheets (see example) and use their mobile devices to help answer the questions. Depending on their version of the activity sheet, groups will either be doing research in the classroom or in the library, moving fluidly from one area to the other.

5. One library instructor remains in the classroom and one instructor goes to the library to help facilitate the quest.

6. For tastiest results, there should be a 10 to 15 minute review and discussion of the library resources, services and supports the students learned about in the quest.

7. You may wish to visit the class again in the following week to give out prizes for best answers, photos, etc. Visiting on the same day would be ideal but it can take at least a week to go through the quest results and select the winners with large class sizes. We like having prizes to reward effort and creativity (eg: best photos, best answers) but results take time to go through. Faculty are often excited to have us back to class the following week for the first 10 minutes to hand out prizes.

ALLERGY WARNINGS

The more detailed instruction you give beforehand, the better the results. If you include instructional videos as part of your quest, emphasize that students will need to watch the videos to answer the questions, as they are a supplement to library instruction. If the library quest is worth a grade or there are prizes to be won, it is usually more successful. We suggest your quest contains interactions with the library's social media. We found not all students were comfortable with this; however, we had great photos submitted on Facebook!

CHEFS' NOTE

The quest engages students much more than a traditional demonstration, and gets them physically and virtually oriented to the library. By embedding how-to videos (e.g.: how to use a discovery layer; APA citation) into the quest, students engage with the library's eLearning support as well. Student feedback has been overwhelmingly positive. Many have enjoyed the simple act of finding a book in the stack, learning about the online resources, or just making new friends.

If faculty are interested in giving out marks or prizes for completion, collect the activity sheets and tally the results. The evaluation for the quest can be simple as marking for completion. If you and the faculty member want to award precise marks, decide on a marking scheme and satisfactory quest answers in advance. We always strive to work

in harmony with the faculty member with respect to how they want, or don't want, to apply credit to student performance.

We are currently transitioning to an online mobile platform that will replace the activity sheets in the Library Quest. Contact us if you're interested in learning more.

ADDITIONAL RESOURCES
Example of the Library Quest Activity Sheet:
http://bit.ly/1RWK2Am

Videos used within the quest:
- http://library.humber.ca/help/apa/books
- https://www.youtube.com/watch?v=0V-C4JZc0r0
- https://www.youtube.com/watch?v=jSpPY1_iBpM

Tic-Tac-Toe and Discover

Christine Elliott, Research & Instruction Librarian, College of Charleston, elliottcr@cofc.edu

NUTRITION INFORMATION

Tic-Tac-Toe is a great way to engage a class of lower and upper-level students with diverse library experiences. Use it to cover essential discovery tool tips before moving on to a useful evaluation worksheet that students can apply to their annotated bibliographies. This is a two-part lesson plan that begins with students competing in a tic-tac-toe game that is customized to highlight resources they can find using the library discovery tool. After completing the game and covering any additional course-related resources, the students work on an annotated bibliography starter, which gives them the chance to focus on their individual research plans, identify databases, and evaluate found articles.

Learning Outcomes

Students will be able to:

- Become critical inquirers.
- Evaluate sources for relevance to assigned/chosen topic.

NUMBER SERVED

Up to 30 students

COOKING TIME

Prep Time: 1 to 2 hours to design and gather questions for the tic-tac-toe game and to generate the 3-Source Annotated Bibliography Starter. This is ideal for a 50 to 75 minute one-shot session.

DIETARY GUIDELINES

Frame: Searching as Strategic Exploration

Knowledge Practices:

- Determine the initial scope of the task required to meet their information needs
- Match information needs and search strategies to appropriate search tools

Dispositions:

- Understand that first attempts at searching do not always produce adequate results
- Realize that information sources vary greatly in content and format and have varying relevance and value, depending on the needs and nature of the search

INGREDIENTS AND EQUIPMENT

- Instructor Station with internet access
- Projector
- Computer lab, with a desktop for each student
- PowerPoint Tic-Tac-Toe Game
- 3-Source Annotated Bibliography Starter (Figure 1)
- Course Research Guide (optional)
- Sample annotated bibliography (optional)

PREPARATION

- This activity works best with a class where an annotated bibliography is required.
- Contact the course instructor to get additional information on the assignment, such as the number of sources and the citation style required.
  - » If possible, get a list of students' topics prior to instruction.
- Determine the students' levels (freshmen, juniors, etc.) so that you can generate tic-tac-toe squares accordingly.
- Build tic-tac-toe game in PowerPoint
  - » The PowerPoint will not be in presentation mode during this exercise. It must stay in the open-editing mode, so that the instructor can freely manipulate the game.
  - » Your PowerPoint must have a minimum of two slides: the introduction and the tic-tac-toe game.
  - » Chose two shapes of your choice to represent the pieces for each team. In my class, I had a gold team and a blue team. The blue team had circles and the gold team had plussigns. Line these shapes up at the top of the slide so that the instructor can easily drag and place the shapes when a team wins a square.
  - » To build the game, insert a 3x3 table onto the designated game

FIGURE 1. 3-Source Annotated Bibliography Starter

YOUR TOPIC: _____

	Academic Article 1	Book/eBook	Academic Article 2
	Source citation	*Source citation*	*Source citation*
Currency • When was the information published?			
Relevance • Is the information appropriate to your needs? • Can the information be related to your topic in a clear, understandable way?			
Authority • Who is the author? • Note credentials, background, experience			
Accuracy • Is this a peer-reviewed source?			
Purpose • Does this source inform or persuade? • Is there bias?			

The 3-Source Worksheet:
- Use a Google account to generate the 3-Source Annotated Bibliography Starter.
- After creating the worksheet, adjust the settings so that anyone with the link can view before making the link available on the course research guide or other platform. Librarians can also print paper copies.

COOKING METHOD

1. After the students arrive for class (they should be sitting at available computer stations and logged in), introduce yourself before dividing the class in half for a fun game of tic-tac-toe.
2. Identify the student on each side who will be the "speaker" for the group before opening the tic-tac-toe PowerPoint presentation on the projector. Inform students that they will all be able to use their computers to search the library website and discovery tool for questions they do not know.
3. The first group will go and select a square on the board. Each group gets 60 seconds to answer the question before the other team gets a chance to answer. If the square has a yes or no question, and the team does not answer correctly, that space will be left blank.
4. The first team to get three in a row wins! If there are spaces left over, reveal them and have the class answer the questions. If there is no winner, then they are all winners; simply go over the remaining squares before declaring a tie.

slide. Type in your questions in each box (the answers to these questions can be included in additional slides or hyperlinked to certain webpages)

» Each box in the table will need a rectangle shape placed over the question. When the game is played, a team picks a box, and you can click on the box and delete it to reveal the question. The box can be any color but transparent.

Example tic-tac-toe boxes:
- List three ways to contact a librarian.
- Is a newspaper article a peer-reviewed source? Can you use it in your paper?
- [Provide a link to a website] Is this website relevant to the topic of [use a topic related to a student topic]? Tell me why you would or wouldn't use it as an academic source.
- Using only the discovery tool, tell me [ask a question related to student topic? How did you find this information?

5. Once the game is completed, provide a brief presentation on how to find articles, books, and other media sources with the discovery tool.
   a. For most classes, I use the topic "women in combat" to do simple and advanced discovery tool searches. Ask the students to help you generate search terms and to evaluate the types of sources that populate the discovery tool results page.
6. It is important to spend some time introducing and/or reviewing the citation format for the class and annotated bibliography assignment.
7. Share the link to the 3-Source Annotated Bibliography Starter and have the students make a copy of the document to complete themselves. Complete an example column so that the students have an idea on how to evaluate an article. Explain to students that the steps they take in evaluating the source in the worksheet will help form the basis of the annotation they need to write for their bibliography.
8. Let students use the rest of their class time to work on the worksheet with their own topics.

ALLERGY WARNINGS
If this class is taught early in the morning, it may be difficult to get students involved with the game. Encourage them with candy. When writing the questions for the game, include a wide range of questions and include items students might not know (like how to determine if the library holds an article in full-text or if it needs to be requested through interlibrary loan), plus simpler questions to keep up morale.

CHEF'S NOTES
This two-part activity is a great way to help lower-level students learn something new, and upper-level students brush up on research strategies. The game lets everyone take part in the teaching process and the worksheet makes it easy for new and seasoned researchers to start finding relevant resources and evaluating them effectively. Many students tend to get overwhelmed by the discovery tool, so it is helpful to remind them how they can refine results while they search.

CLEAN UP
I have used this lesson in a variety of courses. After each session, I invite each student to complete an anonymous, online survey. Inquiries include:
- Overall rating (Poor to Excellent)
- Usefulness of Information (Not Useful to Extremely Useful)
- Summarizing the most important points covered in the session
- Listing points that were not clear during the session
- Suggestions for making the session better

Based on after-session assessments, lower-level and mixed-level classes are more appreciative of the game and worksheet combo while upper-level classes are more interested in spending time on their individual worksheets. Many students have also expressed appreciation for the worksheet because it was easy to use and understand. Many shared with me that they have reused it for other research courses.

Interview Preparation Gumbo

Lateka Grays, Hospitality Librarian, Associate Professor, University of Nevada, Las Vegas, lateka.grays@unlv.edu

NUTRITION INFORMATION

Like any good gumbo, job interview preparation requires a combination of ingredients to create a fully formed stew. This recipe is intended to help students prepare for interviews by exploring and evaluating research about an organization and its industry, in addition to giving them a complete picture about a potential employer.

Learning Outcomes

Students will be able to:

- Use a discovery platform to locate information.
- Develop search strategies to effectively locate information about an organization.
- Apply collected information to evaluate trends and activities of potential employers in order to gain a new perspective about the organization.

NUMBER SERVED

No more than 30 participants (pairs of two will be created for the in-class activity)

COOKING TIME

Pre-workshop preparation for participants: five minutes
Lesson delivery: 55 minutes

DIETARY GUIDELINES

Frame: Searching as Strategic Exploration

Knowledge Practices:

- Determine the initial scope of the task required to meet their information needs.
- Understand how information systems (i.e., collections of recorded information) are organized in order to access relevant information.

Dispositions:

Persist in the face of search challenges, and know when they have sufficient information to complete the information task.

INGREDIENTS & EQUIPMENT

- A computer classroom with Internet access
- Google form or worksheet
- Recipe cards
- Discovery tool tutorial

PREPARATION

- Ask the participants to complete a discovery platform tutorial before they attend the class.
- The level of spiciness or difficulty in locating materials for a specific company will depend upon its organizational structure. Locate at least one of each of the following types of organizations to use as search examples: public, nonprofit, and private.

- Develop a list of useful effective search strategies or keywords that consistently retrieve information about organizations, such as trends, layoffs, and new services.
- Create a Google form to submit answers or print a worksheet for students.

COOKING METHOD

1. Discuss how the type of organization (private, public, nonprofit) affects the nature of the information that students will be able to locate in their research. For example, publicly traded companies are required to report specific types of information to the government; therefore, it will be easier to locate information about this type of company, unlike a privately held company. (15 minutes)
2. Introduce and provide instructions for the hands-on activity (Figure 1). (10 minutes)
3. Students will be given a recipe card (Figure 2) with a question and individually search for news articles or trends about the organization provided, using the discovery platform. Allow 15 minutes for this step. Encourage the students to note the keywords they used in their search. Ask the students to submit their work using the Google form or write their answers using the worksheet.

FIGURE 1. Interview Preparation Gumbo

Purpose: Although, there are many variables that will determine interview success, this workshop will provide participants with a method to begin their preparation for interviews. It will also demonstrate the value of looking beyond a company website to gain additional insight about an organization.

Criteria: Successfully completed activities will identify current materials that enable the interviewee to gain new insight from materials other than the company website.

Tasks: Individually search for news or trend articles about the organization provided by the librarian. You will have 15 minutes to use the discovery system to locate as many articles as you can.

Next, you will take turns being the employer and interviewee. Ask the person sitting next to you the question provided by the librarian. Would you hire the interviewee based on their answer to the question?

Name _____

First and Last Name _____

E-mail _____

Student ID Number _____

Select your assigned question:
- In what areas do you see your given organization expanding, or what obstacles did you discover?
- What do you believe may impact development of new products or services for your organization?

Submit the citations of the articles you located: (Hint: Use the cite feature to cut and paste the article citation below.)

Would you hire the interviewee based on their answer to the question? Why or why not? (Hint: Consider and discuss the quality or reliability of their resources and the depth of material located.)

FIGURE 2. Recipe Card

Recipe — Interview Preparation Gumbo

DIRECTIONS | INGREDIENTS

Your Organization is:

Apple

Your Interview Question is:

In what areas do you see your given organization expanding, or what obstacles did you discover?

guides.library.unlv.edu/gumbo   FROM THE KITCHEN OF *Lateka Grays, Hospitality Librarian*

4. Next, students will take turns being the employer and the interviewee. They will ask each other the question they were given on their recipe card.

5. Then the students will reflect upon the answer provided by their partner, and decide if they would hire them based on their response. Students may judge an answer as acceptable based on relevancy and the resources used. (25 minutes for hands on activity, including the time to search)

6. Bring the group back together to reflect upon the activity. Given the limited amount of time, ask for a volunteer to share their work. This discussion may include suggestions to improve future research. For example, if a student was not hired, the class could walk through a discovery platform search and discuss how to improve the search strategies to the student get the job. (10 minutes)

ALLERGY WARNINGS

To locate organizations, try using company rankings like the Fortune 500, Forbes lists (private, public, charities, etc.), the Nonprofit Times, and trade publication rankings. If available, create an online guide with resources that students can refer to while working on the assignment. Use recipe card templates as a means to distribute the assigned organization and interview question to the students.

CHEF'S NOTES

With the increased publication of literature about embedding career development into the curriculum, this assignment is one that can be adapted for a variety of majors and/or scenarios by librarians who do not specialize in career development.

Discussions from this activity have brought up a variety of issues about the need to try a variety of search strategies to discover relevant resources, the evaluation of resources and the potential bias of some resources, the revelation that they should prepare more for interviews to gain a complete picture of a potential employer, and the surprise about some of the information uncovered about the provided company.

CLEAN UP

The following assessments will apply:
- Students will turn in a worksheet or submit their work via a Google Form. The Google form will allow the librarian to quickly review submissions. When reviewing the submissions, you may look for opportunities to discuss the relevancy of the citations (article, press release, book, etc.) provided. Did the submitted citations effectively answer the question provided by the librarian? Review the hiring decision comments to see how participants reflected upon the relevancy of the information gathered to answer the question.
- If permissible, use a follow-up survey that includes:
  » Name
  » E-mail
  » Classification (freshman, sophomore, junior, senior, graduate student, alumni)
  » Organization you applied to
  » Were you offered a position?
  » How do you feel that your pre-interview preparation increased your understanding of the potential employer?
  » Any additional comments

ADDITIONAL RESOURCES
- LibGuide with assignment resources: http://guides.library.unlv.edu/gumbo
- Company lists:
- Forbes—http://www.forbes.com/lists/
- Fortune 500—http://fortune.com/fortune500/
- The Nonprofit Times—http://www. thenonprofittimes.com/news-articles/ npts-best-nonprofits-to-work-for-2014/
- Recipe card templates (e.g. Avery Design & Print Online templates: http:// dpo.print.avery.com/)

Shopping for the Best Ingredients:
Resource Evaluation and Discovery Tool Searching

Alexandra Hamlett, Information Literacy Librarian, Guttman Community College, CUNY, alexandra.hamlett@guttman.cuny.edu

NUTRITION INFORMATION

The lesson begins with a discussion with the students about their searching habits. Students compile a list of criteria to help them think critically about the accuracy and origins of the information they are consuming. They will evaluate and examine different types of resources which will help them better understand the results generated in a discovery tool search.

Learning Outcomes

Students will be able to:
- Evaluate resources by using different criteria to assess the credibility of the information resource.
- Identify what sources are relevant for their assignment.
- Access the library's discovery tool and navigate its different facets to find appropriate resources for their research assignment.

NUMBER SERVED

20 to 25 students

COOKING TIME

Prep time: 60 minutes
Cooking time: 50 to 75 minutes

DIETARY GUIDELINES

Frame: Searching as a Strategic Exploration

Knowledge Practices:
- Utilize divergent (e.g., brainstorming) and convergent thinking (e.g., selecting the best source) when searching.
- Design and refine search needs and search strategies, based on search results.

Dispositions:
- Understand that first attempts at searching do not always produce adequate results.
- Realize that information sources vary greatly in content and format and have varying relevance and value, depending on the needs and nature of the search.

INGREDIENTS & EQUIPMENT
- White board/flip board
- Examples of different resources (scholarly article, newspaper article, encyclopedia entry)
- Pen/pencil/paper
- Comparing Different Resources handout (Figure 1)
- Internet connection
- Student computers

FIGURE 1. Comparing Different Resources

Directions:
Examine the resource with your group. First, write down all of the things that you notice about the particular article/information in the general observations box. Next, fill out the information in the rest of the chart below.

General observations?	
How long is the article/resource?	
Who wrote the article/resource?	
What is the purpose of the article? Who is it written for?	
What kind of language is used?	
What is the layout/ design? Are there advertisements?	
How did the author(s) get their information for the article?	
How hard is the article to read?	

PREPARATION

- Print out examples of different resources on a particular topic that students will analyze and examine in groups.
- Print copies of the Comparing Different Resources for students.

COOKING METHOD

1. Introduce the librarian prompt: "Today we are going to learn to evaluate the quality of various resources when you are searching for information. This will help you determine whether a resource is relevant and contextual for your research question. By the end of today's lesson, you will be able to identify different types of resources relevant for your research topic. In addition, you will learn how to access and utilize the library's discovery tool to search for relevant resources pertaining to your topic."

2. Begin a class discussion by asking students about their searching behaviors. Ask them what types of questions they ask themselves when deciding what resources will give them the most accurate information that they are seeking.

3. As a class, brainstorm criteria to think about when evaluating the quality of information consumed. Ask students what criteria they think is essential when evaluating the quality of a resource and write the criteria on the whiteboard. This activity should take three to five minutes. The criteria should include: author credentials, accuracy, reputation of publication, currency,

relevance, bias, and purpose.

4. Instruct students to break up into three to four groups to look at different types of information resources. Give each group one information resource (scholarly article, newspaper article, infographic, etc.) and pass out the Comparing Different Resources handout. Have the students spend five minutes or so evaluating the resources based on the evaluation criteria from the class discussion and the handouts.

5. Students present their findings to the class and engage in a class discussion. This should take 15 to 20 minutes.

6. Now that the students have a better understanding of different types of resources, have a brief discussion about the open and closed web. This leads into an explanation of the resources available through the library's website, including the discovery tool.

7. Choose a research topic or use one generated by the students to demonstrate a search within the library's discovery tool.

8. Explain the results page and describe the different result types that are generated.

9. Show the students how to use the facets to limit their results by date, resource type, peer-reviewed, etc.

10. Explain the process of accessing the full-text version of an item, e-mailing the citation information, and saving it to a folder.

11. Allow students to search for resources on their own while circulating the room to assist when needed.

12. Ask the students to briefly reflect on their experience by writing down one 'aha' moment and one 'hmm?' moment from the lesson. They will turn this into the librarian at the end of the session. This portion of the lesson should take 25 to 30 minutes.

ALLERGY WARNINGS

Explain to students that evaluation criteria can be used in all situations where they are looking for reliable information on topics important to them. For example, if they are interested in buying the highest quality, lowest price headphones, it would be advantageous to use good evaluation criteria in order to get the most accurate information.

CHEF'S NOTE

Remind students if they are looking for information on the internet to pay attention to the domain of the web address. Is it a .gov, .edu or .com? These domains can give clues about the origin of the information and the quality of the resource.

CLEAN UP

Through formative assessment, the librarian can monitor students' knowledge of evaluation criteria from the class discussion and again when student groups present the analysis about their assigned resource. The students' reflections from the lesson can help assess the success of the session and help to identify areas where students need further guidance.

A Balanced Plateful:
The Pyramid of Evidence

Rebecca Hewitt, Reference Librarian & Coordinator of Instructional Services, Hartwick College, gordon.rebecca@gmail.com

NUTRITION INFORMATION

The Pyramid of Evidence is a hands-on, active learning exercise which helps students develop a framework with which to evaluate source authority in an academic setting and within discovery tools. It is interactive, rooted in constructivist pedagogy, and has built-in assessment. The lesson is written for first year students and asks them to reflect on their high school research experience, but it can be adapted to students of any level.

Learning Outcomes

Students will be able to:

- Differentiate between sources based on authorship: scholars, professionals, and users.
- Describe the role and significance of editing in the production of research material.
- Independently evaluate sources and rate their authority in a college context.

NUMBER SERVED

Any (25 students per pyramid is the maximum served, but multiple pyramids can be created by a single class)

COOKING TIME

Preparation time is 15 minutes. Lesson length is 45 minutes.

DIETARY GUIDELINES

Frame: Authority is Constructed and Contextual

Knowledge Practices:

- Define different types of authority, such as subject expertise (e.g., scholarship), societal position (e.g., public office or title), or special experience (e.g., participating in a historic event).
- Use research tools and indicators of authority to determine the credibility of sources, understanding the elements that might temper this credibility.

Disposition:

Motivate themselves to find authoritative sources, recognizing that authority may be conferred or manifested in unexpected ways.

INGREDIENTS & EQUIPMENT

- Post-it Notes
- Chalkboard or whiteboard, and appropriate writing implements
- Computer and connected projector (or individual student computers)
- Internet connection

PREPARATION

- Draw one or more large pyramids or stepped pyramids for student use on a whiteboard, chalkboard, easel or wall and label it the "Pyramid of Evidence."
- Post-it notes, two for each student

COOKING METHOD

1. Encourage the students to recall their previous research experiences with a think-pair-share exercise. Ask them to describe to a partner the last school research project they did, and how they found sources of information for that project.
2. After the students are warmed up, ask them to think about the sources they used in that past research project. Ask, for example, "What was in your bibliography or works cited page? Can you name two types of sources that you cited?"
3. Distribute two Post-it Notes to each student, and tell them to write one source that they used for research in the past assignment on each note.
4. The next steps use the students' notes to create a Pyramid of Evidence. Ask the students to think about how much **authority** the sources they wrote down have. For example, you might ask if the students have considered if the information provided by that source is reliable, credible, or trustworthy.

5. Indicating the board with a pyramid or stepped pyramid on it, invite the students to come to the board and place their notes wherever they think they belong on the pyramid, with the **most reliable, or authoritative**, at the top, and the **least authoritative** at the bottom

6. At this point you may have something that looks like an inverted pyramid . A couple of things are clear at this point; students are comfortable with the concept of authority, and they speak fluently of "bias" and "good sources."

7. It is also clear, however, that the high school understanding of authority is very different from a college-level understanding, because in most cases the students' initial pyramid has *Encyclopedia Britannica,* government website or the name of a database at the top. The librarian's challenge is to alter that understanding by adding a new layer, scholarly sources, to the top in a way that resonates with students.

8. Constructivist pedagogy encourages teachers to acknowledge student's current understanding. You can do this by asking students about their sources. For example, you could query them about any resources that you are unfamiliar with.

9. As a transition, explain that a college-level understanding of authority is going to add a new layer to the top of their pyramid. There will be few sources that meet the stringent criteria to make it to the top, that's why the pyramid's top is relatively tiny compared to its base.

10. Describe the college-level pyramid as having roughly three levels. The top of the pyramid, by far the smallest set of resources, has evidence that is created and vetted by scholar/experts. The second level represents evidence and sources written by professionals, e.g. journalists and other professional writers, and edited by professionals. The bottom layer, by far the largest set of sources, has evidence created by users which may or may not be edited (Figure 1).

11. Deploy analogies to improve understanding and recall of the three categories of evidence. Depending on the audience, a college food analogy may aid student comprehension. Items from the bottom of the pyramid are plentiful, inexpensive, but of questionable quality and nutritional value—*Ramen noodles 24/7!* The middle of the pyramid features items that are more selectively available, a little more expensive, and of somewhat better quality—*college dining hall meals!* The few items at the top of the pyramid are available in limited quantities, expensive and high quality—*farm to table restaurant that your family treats you to when they visit!* (Figure 2).

12. To test students' knowledge of the pyramid concept, ask analytical questions such as, "Where does Wikipedia belong on the pyramid?" You may ask the same question with respect to any of the students' Post-it Note sources.

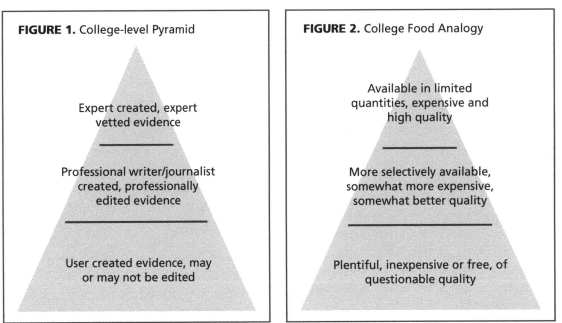

FIGURE 1. College-level Pyramid

Expert created, expert vetted evidence

Professional writer/journalist created, professionally edited evidence

User created evidence, may or may not be edited

FIGURE 2. College Food Analogy

Available in limited quantities, expensive and high quality

More selectively available, somewhat more expensive, somewhat better quality

Plentiful, inexpensive or free, of questionable quality

13. Before moving on to the discovery tool, emphasize that this pyramid is contextual; as described today, it is relevant to college and university projects, which is why it may differ from what students were taught in high school, and it will certainly differ from real world research like buying a car or a house. Ask if there are any further questions about the Pyramid of Evidence.

14. At this point students are ready to search for sources of evidence on their research topics in the discovery tool. When the class moves online, ask the students to do keyword searches on their own individual topics, and give them 10 minutes to explore a variety of searches and results on their own, with yourself and the course professor circulating around the room to lend a hand.

15. After a period of individual work, bring the class's attention back to the front of the classroom. To maximize student attention and engagement, ask students to volunteer a topic, and you perform a live, unrehearsed search in the discovery tool. Refine as necessary to get a set of results that includes a variety of source types.

16. In the discovery tool, the source type icons are very large and prominent—likely to be one of the first things a new user notices on the search results screen. The most frequent source type icons are "academic journal" and "periodical." Ask students the meaning of these terms and where each belongs on the Pyramid of Evidence.

17. As you look at the full text of sources in the discovery tool, note the characteristics discussed when working with the pyramid. If an author's credentials appear on the first page of an article, for example, ask the students why these appear so prominently, and where on the pyramid this article likely belongs based on that evidence. You may ask similar questions with respect to any common characteristic of scholarly and popular sources from the full text of a source, or from the source type icon in your library's discovery tool.

ALLERGY WARNING
To distract students from the computers in front of them, I set up the Pyramid of Evidence board in the rear of the classroom, and conduct the first 15 minutes of the class from there. They pay better attention to the lesson without the distraction of an internet-connected computer in front of them! Having the students rise from their seats to place their Post-it Notes on the pyramid board also encourages active engagement in the lesson.

CHEF'S NOTE
Whenever possible I prefer to do my classes unrehearsed, without canned search examples. Letting the students see my searches occasionally fail shows them that research is difficult and requires iteration, whereas a planned presentation in which everything flows perfectly makes the process look easy and may increase student frustration when they encounter difficulties in the research process. In many cases I solicit student research topics to turn into keyword searches in real time during the class. Students may pay better attention when topics of interest to them are used as examples, and seeing me search with zero results in front of a large group is a moment of comic relief for all of us!

CLEAN UP
With this exercise I prefer real-time assessment via Socratic questioning of students in class. This allows me to know what concepts need further explanation immediately. In most cases I follow up with an e-mail to the class summarizing what we did, providing links to the resources that we used, and including a link to a brief survey, giving students the opportunity to ask questions and/or provide feedback about the class.

Discovering Connections:
A Gourmet Reading Map

Johanna MacKay, Instructional Design Librarian, Skidmore College, jmackay@skidmore.edu; Barbara Norelli, Social Sciences & Instructional Services Librarian, bnorelli@skidmore.edu

NUTRITION INFORMATION

Students use a library discovery tool to find sources that are thematically connected to a shared book/text in order to create a reading map. Similar to a concept map, a reading map (see Additional Resources) visually organizes the themes and topics expressed in a text. The goal of a reading map is to extend the reading experience to focus on themes related to the book. A reading map might include music, films, podcasts, journal or newspaper articles, or even interviews. A discovery tool lends itself to the brainstorming and creation of a reading map by allowing students to explore across databases a variety of subjects and formats. Because the reading can be on any subject or length, this exercise works well for any course. In particular, it is well suited to a first-year experience with an assigned summer reading or a literature course.

Learning Outcomes
Students will be able to:
- Construct a reading map.
- Demonstrate effective search strategies in a discovery tool.
- Identify the various types of sources that may be found with a discovery tool and evaluate them for relevancy.

NUMBER SERVED
Serves up to 20 students with one instructor.

COOKING TIME
Preparation time is approximately one hour to create the handout and prepare the lesson, including consultation with the instructor for text selection. Two to three additional hours may be needed after the lesson to create the interactive reading map (time will vary depending on librarian's familiarity with ThingLink or other tools).
Cook for 50 minutes; may be extended as appropriate.

DIETARY GUIDELINES
Frame 1: Research as Inquiry

Knowledge Practices:
- Organize information in meaningful ways.
- Synthesize ideas gathered from multiple sources.

Disposition:
Consider research as open-ended exploration and engagement with information.

Frame 2: Searching as Strategic Exploration

Knowledge Practices:
- Identify interested parties, such as scholars, organizations, governments, and industries, who might produce information about a topic and then determine how to access that information.
- Utilize divergent (e.g., brainstorming) and convergent (e.g., selecting the best source) thinking when searching.

Dispositions:
- Realize that information sources vary greatly in content and format and have varying relevance and value, depending on the needs and nature of the search.
- Recognize the value of browsing and other serendipitous methods of information gathering.

INGREDIENTS & EQUIPMENT
- Instructor's station with internet access and display capability
- Easel pads or whiteboards and markers
- Computer and internet access for each student team
- Image creation tools (PowerPoint, Paint, Photoshop, Greenshot, SnagIt, etc.)
- ThingLink (interactive image software)

PREPARATION

- Consult with the course instructor on the selection of the text to be used for the reading map.
- Prepare handouts and gather any materials needed for the lesson (e.g., markers, easel pads, etc.).

COOKING METHOD

1. Provide students with the reading map handout. In this instance, the students were asked to help the library create a reading map for the first-year-summer read using the library's discovery tool.
2. Discuss the concept of a reading map.
3. Explain the purpose of a discovery tool including the types of sources students may find.
4. Model finding resources for the reading map using the library discovery tool. (Steps 1–4: 15 minutes)
5. Break the class into teams (ranging from two to five students). Teams brainstorm and map ideas connected with their reading on an easel pad or whiteboard. (10 minutes)
6. Teams search the discovery tool to find two or three resources related to their brainstormed ideas. Students identify these resources on the easel pad or whiteboard. (15 minutes)
7. Student teams share with one another their search strategies and found items while explaining how these items relate to the reading. Librarian collects team findings. (10 minutes)

FIGURE 1. Reading Map Exercise

What is a reading map?

A reading map is similar to a concept map, it visually organizes information related to a specific reading, in this case the book *Einstein's Dreams* by Alan Lightman (first-year summer reading). A reading map is a non-linear depiction of the relationship of ideas expressed in the book. Think about the movie trivia game, Kevin Bacon and 6 degrees of separation, and you've got the idea!

The goal of a reading map is to extend the reading experience to focus on themes related to the book. A reading map might include music, films, podcasts, journal or newspaper articles, or even interviews. Let your imagination go and have fun exploring *Einstein's Dreams* from a different perspective.

Your assignment:

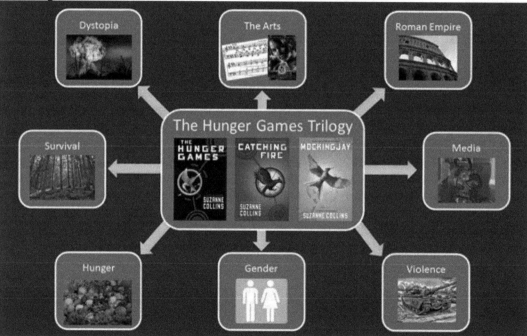

Help the library create a reading map for *Einstein's Dreams*. Use the library's discovery tool to find 2 or 3 specific items and then identify the possible ways in which these items connect to the book.

The completed reading map will be posted to the library's web site.

Worksheet for inspiration: brainstorm your ideas here!

8. After the session, using image software such as PowerPoint, the librarian creates a single reading map by combining the themes explored by the students (Figure 1). Using a tool such as ThingLink, the librarian annotates the image linking the resources found by the students and then shares the reading map with the course instructor and students. For example, we embedded the First Year Experience (FYE) reading map into a LibGuide on the library's website.

ALLERGY WARNING
If you need a popular culture example to explain the connections made in a reading map, mention Kevin Bacon and six degrees of separation. A movie trivia game connecting Kevin Bacon to other actors popularized the six degrees of separation concept, that everyone and everything is related by six or fewer steps. If you need to save time, have students brainstorm and search simultaneously.

CHEF'S NOTE
Searching the discovery tool was shown to the students using an instructor station with internet access and projector. Students used easel pads and markers to brainstorm themes and ideas for the reading maps which were later shared in class. A whiteboard could also be used for this purpose. Students had access to computers in order to conduct their own discovery searches. PowerPoint was used to create the basic reading map image that combined all elements and themes identified by the students. ThingLink (https://www.thinglink.com) was then used by the librarian to annotate the reading map and add interactivity. Alternatively, Prezi, Spicynodes, or any other image technology may be used to create the reading map. If the lesson is used with first-year students consider their summer reading (if applicable) for this activity.

CLEAN UP
While teams search the discovery tool, the librarian circulates to gauge the student's' progress and if necessary guides them to more effective searches. Using the team findings at the end of the lesson, the librarian assesses the shared resources for relevance to the text.

ADDITIONAL RESOURCES
Completed reading map of first-year-read Einstein's Dreams: http://libguides.skidmore.edu/fye.

Using Film as a Starting Point for Information Literacy Instruction

Ilona MacNamara, Associate Librarian, Saint Peter's University, imacnamara@saintpeters.edu

NUTRITION INFORMATION

Films provide a catalyst for conversation and often elicit strong opinions from the observer. Incorporating short film clips in information literacy instruction offers a change from the standard presentation methods. Students coming to the university library for a basic introduction to research strategies do not anticipate beginning the session by viewing a film clip. Showing a specific scene can jumpstart a discussion on how to examine various subjects of interest related to a movie, and to apply this concept to other areas of study.

In this lesson, students watch a five-minute scene. Afterwards, the librarian asks questions to start a conversation and generate participation. The librarian uses the discovery tool, to show students how to access a variety of library resources, such as books, and articles and reviews related to the film. After the demonstration, students conduct individual, hands-on research by using search terms supplied by the librarian based on the film clip. The activity concludes by having students complete a short online survey for assessment.

Learning Outcomes

Students will be able to:

- Use the library's discovery tool, to locate three types of resources that are topic-relevant.

- Generate citations in APA, MLA, or Chicago style using the feature in the discovery tool.
- Learn the name and contact information of the session's librarian in order to obtain assistance with future assignments.

NUMBER SERVED

5 to 20 students

COOKING TIME

Preparation time: 1 hour
Lesson delivery: 50 minutes

DIETARY GUIDELINES

Frame: Searching as Strategic Exploration

Knowledge Practice:
Determine the initial scope of the task required to meet their information needs.

Disposition:
Seek guidance from experts, such as librarians, researchers, and professionals.

INGREDIENTS & EQUIPMENT

- Computer lab with internet connection equipped with instructor's workstation, projector and screen
- Student computers
- Short film clip for viewing in class

- Online questionnaire for assessment

PREPARATION

- The librarian should choose a visually interesting or evocative movie available on DVD, which contains a captivating scene lasting no longer than five minutes. Before the lesson, the DVD is fast forwarded to the selected film clip.
- Prior research needs to be done to ensure that students will be able to locate a variety of library resources related to the film.
- Develop a short online questionnaire that assesses the learning outcomes and is administered at the conclusion of the activity.

COOKING METHOD

1. The first five minutes of the lesson focuses on showing a film clip. This particular exercise showcases a scene from the movie *House of Flying Daggers* directed by Zhang Yimou, released in 2004. The students view the Echo Game scene, which is unexpected, visually dynamic and engages students in a conversation/icebreaker.
2. For the next 15 minutes, the librarian conducts sample searches based on concepts related to the film clip, using the discovery tool. Explain to students

that it is a single gateway that simultaneously searches the library's extensive collection of print and electronic resources. In addition point out that each record contains a citation feature, which generates APA, MLA, or Chicago style citations. Be sure to stress that generated citations may require minor edits to be accurate and it is recommended that students verify their citations to make sure they are correct.

3. Students are given 20 minutes to use the discovery tool to locate any three of the resources listed: a biography—book or article, a newspaper article, a peer-reviewed article, a review of the film, a print book, and an e-book, and then generate a citation in APA, MLA or Chicago style for each of their choices.

4. The librarian provides search terms to expedite the activity, and is available to assist students during the exercise. The following terms give students the opportunity to research topics of personal interest with artistic, biographical, cultural, or historical perspectives: *House of Flying Daggers*, Tang Dynasty, Zhang Yimou, Zhang Ziyi, Wushu, Chinese cinema, Chinese culture and women in Chinese films.

5. The concluding 10 minutes are devoted to a brief discussion of the lesson. Students complete a short online survey for assessment and the librarian provides his/her contact information for future assistance.

FIGURE 1. Library Instruction Survey

Thank you for providing feedback. Your answers will assist in making enhancements to library instruction.

1. My student classification is:
   - ❑ Freshman
   - ❑ Sophomore
   - ❑ Junior
   - ❑ Senior

2. Date of instruction: _____

3. Course title & name of professor: _____

4. Librarian's name: _____

5. I visit the library to (check all that apply):
   - ❑ study
   - ❑ use the computers
   - ❑ make photocopies
   - ❑ ask for research assistance
   - ❑ check out books
   - ❑ use Reserve items
   - ❑ This is my first visit
   - ❑ Other: _____

6. I have had previous library instruction.
   - ❑ Yes
   - ❑ No

7. After today's instruction, I feel confident in using the university library's discovery tool.
   - ❑ Strongly Agree
   - ❑ Agree
   - ❑ Neutral
   - ❑ Disagree
   - ❑ Strongly Disagree
   - ❑ Comment: _____

8. List three useful tips you learned during the session: _____

9. As a result of this session, are you more likely to begin research by using Google or the library's discovery tool?
   - ❑ Library's discovery tool
   - ❑ Google
   - ❑ Comment: _____

10. What is one thing you would change about the session?_____

ALLERGY WARNINGS

Adhere to a strict time schedule. Move the lesson along to ensure goals are met.

CHEF'S NOTE

This activity is intended for students to explore the library's discovery tool, and to recognize the countless resources available in the collection. It is open to numerous film genres. Select a scene that is visually appealing or has a strong narrative and is no longer than five minutes. In addition, this exercise is helpful in cases where students do not have an assigned topic, and the session is intended to be a one-shot introduction to library resources.

CLEAN UP

Online survey is distributed to students consisting of qualitative and quantitative questions (Figure 1). The results help in determining whether the goals of the lesson have been met and are used to make enhancements to the lesson.

ADDITIONAL RESOURCES

- Costanzo, William V. *Great Films and How to Teach Them.* Urbana: NCTE, 2004.
- Costanzo, William V. *World Cinema through Global Genres.* Chichester: John Wiley & Sons, 2014.
- *Film Education.* U.K. Film Industry, 13 Apr. 2013. Web. 17 Dec. 2015. <www.filmeducation.org>.

First-Year-Seminar Discovery Tool Casserole

Henri Mondschein, Manager of Information Literacy, California Lutheran University, mondsche@callutheran.edu

NUTRITION INFORMATION

First-year seminar students will explore a topic using the library's discovery layer and learn how this tool provides access to sources in various formats including books, e-books, articles, and streaming video. Students will also limit their results to a specific format such as e-book or video. In addition, students will learn how to place a print book on hold. The students will work in small groups and together explore the functionality of the discovery tool by responding to guiding questions provided on a handout.

Learning Outcomes

Students will be able to:

- Brainstorm keywords in order to construct a search strategy to retrieve information from the library on a research topic.
- Determine how to limit search results in order to retrieve only books or e-books.
- Identify other types of sources besides books and e-books (e.g. articles, streaming video) in order to characterize information into different formats.

NUMBER SERVED

25 students

COOKING TIME

Prep time: About 30 minutes. This includes reviewing the lesson plan, photocopying worksheets, and setting up the computer lab or active learning classroom.
Lesson Delivery: 50 minutes. This includes 20 minutes for students to complete the activity and about 10 minutes to call on teams to demonstrate what each group found.

DIETARY GUIDELINES

Frame: Searching as Strategic Exploration

Knowledge Practices:

- Determine the initial scope of the task required to meet their information needs.
- Match information needs and search strategies to appropriate search tools.
- Utilize divergent (e.g., brainstorming) and convergent (e.g., selecting the best source) thinking when searching.

Dispositions:

- Understand that first attempts at searching do not always produce adequate results.
- Realize that information sources vary greatly in content and format and have varying relevance and value, depending on the needs and nature of the search.
- Recognize the value of browsing and other serendipitous methods of information gathering.

INGREDIENTS & EQUIPMENT

- Handouts providing students with activity instructions
- Instructions for librarian
- Rubric for scoring student responses (see Figure 1)

PREPARATION

- Reserve active learning classroom
- Set up laptops or computers
- Photocopies of handouts for distribution

COOKING METHOD

1. **Script:** "Everyone in this room knows how to find information on the Web. We also know that you can't trust everything you find on the Web. As you begin your academic experience at <name of institution> your professors will expect you to include trustworthy sources in your class projects. Instead of relying entirely on the Web for information, you will also be using some of the library's research sources. Today, we are going to let you explore the library's discovery tool to find information on a topic. The discovery tool works like a search engine such as Google except that the

Figure 1. Exploring Library Tools Activity Scoring Rubric

Task	1. Beginning	2. Developing	3. Proficient
Discusses how to begin research using the discovery tool. Lists precise keywords	Student provides cursory or unclear steps on how to begin using the discovery tool. Does not list keywords or provides imprecise keywords.	Student describes some of the steps one takes in using the discovery tool. May list some precise keywords.	Student clearly describes steps one takes in beginning discovery tool search. Lists sufficient and precise keywords.
Describes steps for limiting results to print books only	Student provides unclear or inaccurate steps to limiting results to print books.	Student describes to some extent correct steps to limiting results to print books	Student clearly describes steps to limit results to print books.
Describes steps for limiting results to e-books only	Student provides unclear or inaccurate steps to limiting results to e-books.	Student describes to some extent correct steps to limiting results to e-books.	Student clearly describes steps to limit results to e-books.
Provides steps for limiting results to articles.	Student provides unclear or inaccurate steps for limiting results to articles.	Student provides to some extent correct steps for limiting results to articles.	Student provides clear and complete steps for limiting results to articles.
Describes steps involved in reserving a print book from the library.	Student provides unclear, inaccurate or limited steps for reserving or placing a hold on a print book.	Student provides adequate steps for reserving or placing a hold on a print book. Includes at least one step such as clicking on the Place Hold button.	Student provides clear steps for reserving or placing a hold on a print book. Includes examples such as clicking on the Place Hold button and clicking Submit.

sources it finds are found within our library and outside libraries rather than the Web. You'll also be looking at some of our many databases and decide on a few that you can also use to research a specific topic."

2. Divide students into small groups of three to four. Briefly show them the library page, and the links for the research guides and how to access the discovery tool but allow them to explore functionality of the discovery tool in their groups.

3. Display the research question on the screen. Also distribute the worksheet that describes the research topic and the tasks that students must complete as they explore the discovery tool. The worksheet provides guiding questions for the students to discuss in their teams and answer (Figure 2).

4. In their groups review the worksheet and give the students 15 minutes to complete the task in their teams.

5. Have a volunteer from each group demonstrate what they did and explain their response to one of the worksheet questions.

ALLERGY WARNINGS

Encourage discussion during the student demonstrations by asking "how" and "why" questions that promote reflection and critical thinking related to the Framework dispositions outlined. Other questions to encourage reflection and reinforcement of learning include: What did you learn

---

FIGURE 2. Exploring the Discovery Tool

This group activity will get you started in exploring the functions and features of the Library's discovery tool. The discovery tool is similar to a search engine such as Google except that the sources it retrieves are found within the library and outside libraries rather than the World Wide Web. Your librarian will point out where you can find the discovery tool, but it will be ut to you to learn how it works. This activity will be completed in your groups and requires that you collaborate with your team members. Each team will complete one worksheet which will be collected at the end of this session. Your research topic is:

"How does Posttraumatic Stress Disorder or PTSD impact the lives of military veterans?"

Your task is to find some relevant library resources on this topic. Follow the prompts below.

1. **Go to the Library's homepage and discuss in your group how you would begin your research using the discovery tool. Discuss keywords you might use in your research and list those here:**
2. **How would you limit your search results to see only print books in the library? Explain:**
3. **How would you limit your results to see only e-books? Explain:**
4. **How would you limit your results to view only articles? Explain:**
5. **What other types of sources appear in your search results? Explain:**
6. **What are the steps involved in reserving a print book from the library? Explain:**

---

from this activity? How is the discovery tool similar to a search engine? In what ways is it different? What are some advantages of using e-books? Why can't one download and keep an entire e-book indefinitely? Why do you suppose there is a limit on the number of pages one can download or print from an e-book? How would you use video files in an assignment or presentation?

CHEF'S NOTE

It is important to make sure there is enough time to complete this activity, as the work the students do in their small groups or teams promotes engagement and the highlighted knowledge practices (e.g. creating search strategies, brainstorming, and selecting the best sources). The questions will instruct students to discuss keywords, for example, or to limit their searches to a specific format. The librarian then requires

each team to share and demonstrate for the class for instance, how they performed a keyword search while displaying the search results on a screen for the class to view. At the conclusion of the session, the worksheets are collected by the librarian. The activity works best in active learning classroom where students can work in small groups and display their search results on a screen for the entire class to view.

CLEAN UP

Collect the worksheets from each table. Use the rubric to score the responses (Figure 1). The scores will provide the librarian with assessment data on how well the class performed and learned the skills and concepts necessary to begin researching a topic using the discovery tool.

Discovering Inquiry Workshop

Mark Robison, Research Services Librarian, Valparaiso University, mark.robison@valpo.edu

NUTRITION INFORMATION

Upper-level students will use a discovery tool to locate scholarly articles. With chef's guidance, they will explore the structure and purposes of two key components of an article: the introduction and the literature review. Through interaction and discussion, students will learn that research is about asking questions. Students will also use a discovery tool to unearth a network of scholarly literature, starting with the article they found, in order to understand the key role citation networks play in becoming a mature researcher.

Learning Outcomes

Students will be able to:

- Explain how, within most scholarly articles, the introductions and literature reviews are structured to identify an unresolved question within a field and then to explain how that article will contribute to answering that question.
- Use discovery tools in order to unearth networks of scholarly literature.

NUMBER SERVED

8 to 30 upper-level students. Number will depend on the size of the computer lab; at least one computer is needed per pair of students.

COOKING TIME

Prep time: 45 minutes
Lesson delivery: 50 minutes

DIETARY GUIDELINES

Frame 1: Research as Inquiry

Knowledge Practice:
Formulate questions for research based on information gaps or on reexamination of existing, possibly conflicting, information.

Disposition:
Consider research as open-ended exploration and engagement with information.

Frame 2: Scholarship as Conversation

Knowledge Practice:
Identify the contribution that particular articles, books and other scholarly pieces make to disciplinary knowledge.

Disposition:
Recognize they are often entering into an ongoing scholarly conversation and not a finished one.

INGREDIENTS & EQUIPMENT

- One whole computer lab, peeled, where students can log in
- One cup of fresh computer station and projector, for chef's use
- One batch of handouts, one per student
- A dash of extra pens

PREPARATION

- Familiarize yourself with the discovery tool's Advanced Search features.
- Review a scholarly article so that the structures of introductions and literature reviews are fresh in mind.
- Make any necessary changes to terminology on worksheet (Figure 1) to match chef's discovery tool of choice. For example, limiting the search to "Abstract" may not be an option in the Advanced Search feature in your discovery tool. In this case, "Title" or "Full Text" could be suitable alternatives; chefs should anticipate how such edits will cause students' search results to be narrower or broader, respectively.
- Make copies of the worksheet.
- Get to the classroom early so cooking can begin on time.

COOKING METHOD

1. Begin the workshop with a brief overview of the discovery tool and its Advanced Search features.
2. Introduce first student task: Working in pairs, students will follow the instructions for Part 1 of accompanying worksheet to search for and access a scholarly journal article, using the discovery tool. Their chosen article must include an introduction and a formal literature

review. In their pairs, students will skim the introduction and literature review and then answer the questions on the accompanying worksheet.

3. After the groups have finished, reconvene the class and lead them in a discussion of the articles they read and the structure of the article. In this discussion, be sure to touch on how much of research consists of identifying gaps in the literature and posing new questions.

4. Introduce second student task: Working in pairs, students will follow the instructions for Part 2 of worksheet to locate two of the sources cited in their articles. They will first locate the exact articles cited, and then attempt to locate additional sources that cite these articles.

5. After the groups have finished, reconvene the class for a discussion about why scholars cite one another and the value of tapping into this network of citations when doing research. Let them discuss their successes and failures; clarify questions as necessary.

6. Wrap up with a recap of the topics covered.

ALLERGY WARNINGS

This recipe can quickly become "meta." Students will need careful explanation that they are moving between several layers of the citation web. Visual illustrations could be helpful. The discovery tool will not locate all the article titles searched. Chef should reassure anxious students who are struggling.

FIGURE 1. Discovering Inquiry Workshop

Part 1: Research Means Asking Questions
Work with one partner. Navigate to the discovery tool's Advanced Search page. In the first text box, type *Literature Review* and select "Full Text" from the drop-down menu. In the second text box, enter a topic that interests you (e.g. voting behavior, gender, nuclear nonproliferation) and select "Abstract" from the drop-down menu. Click Search, and then limit your results to Journal Articles. Choose one article that you can view full-text. Open the article. After skimming through the first few pages, answer the following questions with your partner.

What is the main topic of the article?
In the **introduction**, what kinds of sources are cited?
What happens in the article's introduction? What purpose does the introduction serve?
In the **literature review**, what kinds of sources are cited? Are these different from the kinds of sources used in the introduction?
What happens in the literature review? What purpose does the literature review serve?

FIGURE 1. Discovering Inquiry Workshop (continued)

Part 2: Scholarship Means Citing Other People

When they write, scholars cite one another for many reasons: to support their claims; to establish credibility; to identify unresolved problems; etc. Tapping into this **network of citations** is a great way to find additional high-quality sources for a research project. You can use the discovery tool to tap into this network of citations, using the steps below.

Return to your article's literature review. In the spaces below, write the titles of any two journal articles cited in that literature review.

Article #1 Title:

Article #2 Title:

Navigate back to the Advanced Search page. Clear all the search fields and start fresh. In the first text box, enter the full title of Article #1. From the drop-down menu, select "Title" and then click Search. Did the discovery tool find Article #1? Does the library have access to it?

Repeat these steps, entering the full title of Article #2. Again, do a "Title" search. Did the discovery tool find Article #2? Does the library have access to it?

Now you can make a small change that will uncover other articles that cite these Articles #1 & #2. Return to the Advanced Search page. Change the drop-down menu to "Full Text" or "All Text." In the text box, enter the full title of Article #1, and **wrap it in quotation marks**. Click Search. This time, the discovery tool should find other sources that cite that article in their document. Take a few notes about the kinds of sources the discovery tool found.

Repeat the steps above using the title of Article #2. Do a "Full Text" or "All Text" search. What kinds of sources did the discovery tool find?

What is the difference between "Full Text" searching and "Title" searching?

CHEF'S NOTE

Expect a lot of "Ah-ha!" moments from students as they realize how straightforward research can be once they know the ropes.

CLEAN UP

Work with the instructor to review a selection of students' final projects, to determine whether students tapped into networks of peer-reviewed scholarship.

A Case of the Research Munchies:
Evaluating Which Resource Will Hit the Spot

Brandon West, Social Sciences Librarian, SUNY Geneseo, westb@geneseo,edu; Michelle Costello, Head of Instructional Services, SUNY Geneseo, costello@geneseo.edu

NUTRITION INFORMATION

First-year students need more than just instruction on the different types of library resources and how to use them. They need to learn how to think about a topic and critically analyze the multifaceted nature of their research. This lesson sets students on the path to success by engaging them in hands-on, active learning activities. Given the introductory nature to this lesson, it can easily be adapted for students in grades 9 to 12.

Learning Outcomes

Students will be able to:

- Explore various sources using the discovery tool in order to assess their information need.
- Determine the scope of their information needs by brainstorming multiple perspectives in order to create a research statement.
- Match information needs and search strategies using the discovery tool in order to locate an appropriate resource.

NUMBER SERVED

Ideal class size is 20 to 30 students, although lesson is adaptable to smaller or larger classes.

COOKING TIME

Prep Time: 30 to 45 minutes
Lesson: 75 minutes. Lesson can be adapted from generic to specific contexts.

DIETARY GUIDELINES

Frame 1: Research as Inquiry

Knowledge Practice:
Use various research methods, based on need, circumstance, and type of inquiry.

Disposition:
Seek multiple perspectives during information gathering and assessment.

Frame 2: Searching as Strategic Exploration

Knowledge Practice:
Match information needs and search strategies to appropriate search.

Disposition:
Exhibit mental flexibility and creativity.

INGREDIENTS & EQUIPMENT

- Computer access for all students
- Instructor station
- Whiteboard or equivalent
- Recording sheet, Google Doc or other recording software, such as Padlet, for students to record their work.

PREPARATION

- Design a research topic for student exploration.
- Create a recording sheet or Google Doc (or other recording software, such as Padlet) for student responses (Figure 1).
- Decide on a strategy for grouping students before the lesson.

COOKING METHOD

Part One—Activate Prior Knowledge
Warm-up Activity (5 minutes)

1. Ask students how many of them have shopped online before.
2. Have the students search for a pair of shoes.
3. Students will spend a couple minutes searching websites of their choice.
4. Have students report out on the strategies they used.
5. Write a few strategies on the whiteboard for them to refer to later.

Part Two—Exploring the Discovery Tool
Direct Instruction (5 minutes)

FIGURE 1. A Case of the Research Munchies Recording Sheet

Part Two—Exploring the Discovery Tool

Topic: _____

Search Terms used:

Discovery Tool

# of results:

Types of items found in the database:

What are some of the ways to limit your results or make them more relevant?

Strengths (what do you like about this discovery tool?):

Weaknesses (what's confusing/what's difficult about this discovery tool?):

1. Explain the student's research assignment, project, or task. Draw parallels between the warm-up activity with conducting academic research.
2. Display and introduce the discovery tool. Tell the students that this is a good place to start their research (as Google was a good place to look for shoes).
3. Explain that they will be exploring our library discovery tool to see the kinds of items it contains and to test out the filters/limiters.
4. Provide a brief demo of the discovery tool.

Student Practice (10 minutes)
1. Break students into small groups of 3 to 4.
2. Students will perform a sample search on the research topic the librarian creates using the library's discovery tool.
3. They will work in groups to evaluate the features, strengths, and weaknesses of the discovery tool.
4. Students will record their findings on a recording sheet (or a Google Doc/Padlet).

Check for Understanding (5 minutes)
1. Have students share with the larger group what they discovered about the tool.
2. Ask students additional questions about the discovery tool that they may have not mentioned.

FIGURE 1. A Case of the Research Munchies Recording Sheet (continued)

Part Three—Forming a Research Question & Statement

Fill out the following chart based upon your topic:

When/Time	Where/Place
What/Event	Who/Person

What are some of the different perspectives might you consider?

Choose at least one perspective and note the kinds of questions a person in the given perspective might ask?

Research Question (RQ): _____

Reflecting on your RQ:
- Is my RQ something that I am curious about and that others might care about?
- Does it present an issue on which I can take a stand?
- Does my RQ put a new spin on an old issue, or does it try to solve a problem?
- Is my RQ too broad, too narrow, or OK?
- Is my RQ measurable? What type of information do I need? Can I find actual data to support or contradict a position?

Use your question to create a search strategy

Concept 1: _____OR _____ OR _____

AND

Concept 2: _____ OR _____ OR _____

AND

Concept 3: _____OR _____ OR _____

Part Four—Independent Searching & Conclusion

Find either a book or an article that addresses your research question.

BOOK:	**ARTICLE:**
Title:	Article Title:
Author(s):	Author(s):
Publisher:	Journal Title:
Place of Publication	Vol: _____ Issue: _____
Year:	Date: _____ Page #s: _____
Call Number:	

Part Three—Forming a Research Question and Statement

Direct Instruction (5 minutes)

1. Explain that in the past the students may have started with a thesis statement when searching for material. However, for college assignments it is easier to start with a research question.
2. Briefly walk students through the process of creating a research question (RQ) by reviewing criteria for a RQ.
3. Discuss how an issue often has multiple perspectives and how it is necessary to consider these perspectives when developing a RQ.

Student Practice (10 minutes)

1. In their groups, students will brainstorm ideas related to different perspective for the research topic and record their answer on the RQ chart (see recording sheet).
2. Bring the class together and discuss the different perspectives related to the research topic.
3. Now have the groups develop a question based around one of the perspectives generated.
4. Students will record their questions in the recording sheet or Google Doc.

Direct Instruction (5 Minutes)

1. Having the right question makes it easier to find the right keywords to enter into the database.
2. Explain that now that they have a research question, they will need to

decide which keywords they can use to get the best results from the discovery tool.

3. Show students how to break out the main concepts out of a research question and offer them an explanation about using synonyms.

Student Practice (5 minutes)

1. Students will develop keywords for their research question and record them on the recording sheet or Google Doc.

2. Circulate around the room while students work.

Part Four—Independent Searching and Conclusion
Student Practice (20 minutes)

1. Give the students time to use the discovery tool to locate a library resource they believe is appropriate for their research question.

2. Students will record why and how they will use the resource to answer their research question.

Wrap-up Activity (5 minutes)

1. Ask the students "What strategies have they learned during class for finding research?"

2. Call on students to respond. Make sure to point out any key ideas they may have missed.

3. Remind students that they can use these strategies for any of their projects/assignments and remind them that librarians are here to help.

ALLERGY WARNINGS
While all four parts work well together, you may choose which ones to include based on student prior knowledge, time allotment, or assignment requirements. It is best to tailor the sample topic to a specific assignment or theme of the course. While we value integrating technology into our instruction, this lesson can be taught without the use of educational technologies.

CHEFS' NOTES
Be flexible when teaching this lesson; students may need more time in one part than in another. This session works best as collaboration between the instructor and librarian. Discussing expectations and getting student topics beforehand help make the lesson more targeted toward students' need. You can tailor this lesson to specific databases in lieu of the discovery tool.

CLEAN UP
Assessment is holistically integrated throughout this lesson. Each time students complete a task in each step of the lesson they will record their responses. These responses are shared with the librarian and class at large, which serve as both formative assessment and summative assessment. In addition, students are participating in discussion throughout the lesson, which serves as formative assessment.

5. REGIONAL FARE
lesson plans for international students, faculty, and K–12

Introducing Research Basics:
History Day Programming for Local High Schools

Megan Allison, Library Support Senior, Bailey/Howe Library, University of Vermont, megan.f.allison@gmail.com

NUTRITION INFORMATION

High school students participating in state History Day competitions are expected to select a research topic based on a theme, find primary and secondary sources of information, and prepare a final project for the competition. By collaborating with local high school teachers, academic librarians have an opportunity to introduce students to university libraries, reference services, and primary source collections, often for the first time. The discovery tool is a key element of this lesson plan and is introduced in a tutorial before the students visit the library. On the day of the visit, discovery tool concepts are reviewed in a demonstration. Students are then asked to "kick it up a notch" by learning how to critically review their search results, broaden and narrow their searches, and target both primary and secondary sources with the discovery tool. Instruction is wrapped up with students learning how some of the discovery tool concepts can be carried over and used in their school database searches.

Learning Outcomes
Students will be able to:
- Evaluate and revise their searches based on the kinds of results they are getting.
- Formulate queries in the discovery tool that target primary and secondary sources.
- Recognize the many ways that librarians can help them with their research.

NUMBER SERVED
20 to 40 students per a visit (or as many as your classroom can hold).

COOKING TIME
Prep time: 4 hours. There is an initial time investment in this project due to the prep work involved. The good news is that once these building blocks are created, you can always recycle them for future History Day visits.

Cooking time: 30 minutes of instruction and 2 hours of research time where students can visit primary source collections, talk research with a reference librarian, or explore the library's various research tools and resources.

DIETARY GUIDELINES
Frame 1: Searching as Strategic Exploration

Knowledge Practice:
Design and refine needs and search strategies as necessary, based on search results.

Dispositions:
- Understand that first attempts at searching do not always produce adequate results.
- Seek guidance from experts, such as librarians, researchers, and professionals.

Frame 2: Authority is Constructed and Contextual

Knowledge Practice:
Define different types of authority, such as subject expertise (e.g., scholarship), societal position (e.g., public office or title), or special experience (e.g., participating in a historic event).

Disposition:
Motivate themselves to find authoritative sources, recognizing that authority may be conferred or manifested in unexpected ways.

INGREDIENTS & EQUIPMENT
- Research guide
- Discovery tool tutorial
- Pre-visit assignment (Figure 1)
- Technology equipped classroom for instruction and research space
- Temporary network login information

FIGURE 1. Getting Started on Your Research
Please take 15 to 20 minutes to complete this assignment before you come to the library.

1. What is your topic: _____
2. Find your topic in a Subject Encyclopedia.
   - You can look at encyclopedias at your school or local library.
   - Or, if you want to look at encyclopedias online, many school and public libraries have subscriptions to online reference resources/subject encyclopedias.
3. Start developing keywords by filling in the table below:

	Answer	Is there another way to phrase this term?
Note **terms** used in the encyclopedia article which refer to your topic.		Are there other synonyms for these terms?
Identify key **people** and **organizations** related to your topic		Do these people go by any other names, pseudonyms, organizational names or acronyms?
When does your topic take place, is there a date range or dates of specific events?		How else could you search for this date: with the specific date, the decade, the century, the era?
Where does your topic take place?		What is the city, state, region, country?

4. All of the above answers can be search terms. Try using different combinations of these terms to search an online subject encyclopedia two more times. If you find other good search terms, add them to your keyword list.
5. Complete the Discovery Tool Tutorial.
6. Use your search terms to search the Discovery Tool two times. Note a resource you'd like to look at when you get to the library: _____
7. Using the Discovery tool, look at the record for the resource you noted above. Is there information in this record that can inform your keyword list? Try looking at the book/article descriptions and the subjects listed in the record. Update your keyword list with new terms from the resource record that may improve your searches.

8. Record issues or questions that you'd like to ask the librarians when you get here:

REMEMBER, the quality of your research improves as you learn more about your topic. As you go, you may find that some combinations of search terms work better than others or you may find new search terms that can improve your searches. Don't settle on the first resource you find, keep looking until you find good resources for your topic.

- Librarians managing primary source collections who are interested in cross-departmental collaboration and instruction (for example, a government documents librarian or an archivist).
- Reference/Instruction librarians to answer reference questions

PREPARATION

- Once a teacher expresses interest in a visit, get some specifics about when the visit will take place, how many students will be participating, and the kinds of research skills the students might need help with. You should also request a list of student topics.
- Work with IT to set up temporary network access for the students.
- Develop a research guide. This could offer a variety of information, but be sure to include the following:
  - » Prep work for the students to complete before their visit. For example, completion of the pre-visit assignment and any advance planning for technology needs (like printing or saving information).
  - » How students can take information with them (i.e. copying/scanning/ e-mailing/taking pictures/checking out books).
  - » An introduction and a link to the discovery tool.
  - » Recommendations for databases or other subject guides.
  - » Instruction related to authority and iterative research.
  - » Information about your library's pri-

mary source collections: what they are, how to find materials, and how to visit.

» Information for teachers wanting to set up a visit.

- Develop a pre-visit assignment to introduce the discovery tool that demonstrates how students can begin developing keywords:

  » Students should get a sense of how their research strategy may improve as they learn more about their topic.

  » Students should complete the discovery tool tutorial and try a few discovery tool searches.

  » Students should begin a keyword list that is informed by the information they find in their initial searches using the discovery tool.

- Consult with librarians managing primary source and government information collections. Share the student topics that relate to their collections, and collaborate on the best way for students to work with those collections.

- Request volunteers to field research questions. One reference librarian for every twenty students seems to work.

- Prepare the classroom:

  » Confirm you have enough chairs/computers

  » Write important information/hints on the whiteboard, for example:

    ◆ Login information for the computers

    ◆ Tips for searching for people/

phrases/synonyms/etc.

◆ Tips for finding primary sources with the discovery tool

COOKING METHOD

1. Build on ideas presented in the pre-visit assignment, the discovery tool tutorial, and the subject guide. Plan to spend about 30 minutes on instruction.

2. Review how to use the discovery tool. Talk about clues for identifying when a search misses the mark. Show students how to broaden or narrow their searches.

3. Demonstrate how to find primary sources using the discovery tool. Due to the emphasis on getting both primary and secondary sources for the History Day project, and because primary source collections are available in the library, students will likely be very interested in developing searches targeted at primary sources.

4. Demonstrate how to find and use a database. You can frame this in terms of skills that translate from the discovery tool to the database, such as similar ways to refine your results.

5. Offer examples of the kinds of help that reference librarians can provide, from a quick discussion about research strategies to finding a book in the stacks. These new users may have no idea what subject librarians can do.

6. Don't forget to offer information about the logistics of the day's visit, such as where to find a reference librarian, how

to log on to the network, visiting other departments, etc.

7. After the presentation, students can begin using library resources. Reference librarians should be available to assist or answer questions as needed. Students with applicable topics can also visit primary source collections at this point, such as an archive or government repository.

ALLERGY WARNINGS

Consider what the students will and will not have access to once they leave your library:

- Will they be able to check out books?
- Are there places they can scan or copy, and how much do these options cost?
- Are there other alternatives for taking information with them, could they take pictures with a tablet or smartphone?
- What about information pulled from databases? E-mailing information directly from a database probably won't work. It is likely that the e-mail will only include a link to the information, and the students won't have access to the network after they leave the library. Show them how to save the information and e-mail it to themselves.

CHEF'S NOTE

The pre-visit assignment is integral to this lesson plan as it introduces the discovery tool, urges students to develop keywords, and reminds students that research is iterative, search terms may evolve, and the best resource is not always the first resource you find. Laying this foundation sets the stage for the actual library visit, where students are likely to be very interested in targeting primary sources in their discovery tool searches, and in visiting primary source collections or government information.

CLEAN UP
After the visit, consider working with the student's teacher to do a short student survey. Finding out what the students' overall impressions of the experience were, what they learned and what they are still confused about will lay the groundwork for continuing to improve this experience and its outcomes.

ADDITIONAL RESOURCES
Sample Research Guide: http://research-guides.uvm.edu/historyday/home

Subject Term Soup (with Vocabulary Garnish)

Emily Crist, Library Assistant Professor, University of Vermont, ecrist@uvm.edu; Lauren Strachan, MA Student, Applied Linguistics, Concordia University, laurenhirdrutter@gmail.com

NUTRITION INFORMATION

This lesson plan, collaboratively developed from the fields of academic librarianship and applied linguistics, targets the information literacy and language skills of English language learners (ELLs). Specifically, the lesson emphasizes the understanding of subject terms as tools for modifying and refining an information search in a discovery tool. By attending to subject terms, learners also practice word association skills through the thematic grouping of related words and concepts. These skill sets combine to reinforce familiarity with scholarly source formats by helping learners understand the relationship between subject terms and abstracts and eventually produce sample abstracts of their own.

Learning Outcomes

Students will be able to:

- Produce searches using a discovery tool.
- Recognize and categorize subject terms related to a topic.
- Select subject terms based on their topic of inquiry.
- Use word association techniques to build vocabulary.
- Model academic writing through the creation of abstracts based on subject terms.

NUMBER SERVED

10 or more (as computer lab allows)

COOKING TIME

Prep time: 30 minutes
Lesson: 90 minutes

DIETARY GUIDELINES

Frame: Research as Inquiry

Knowledge Practice:
Organize information in meaningful ways.

Disposition:
Value persistence, adaptability, and flexibility and recognize that ambiguity can benefit the research process.

INGREDIENTS & EQUIPMENT

- Computers with access to discovery tool
- Whiteboard for brainstorming
- Article abstracts
- Ideas for keywords

PREPARATION

- To prepare, gather a set of abstracts and corresponding subject terms (one for each pair of students) appropriate for the ELLs' reading comprehension.
- Choose and cut up sample subject terms that learners will turn into an abstract of their own.
- Ideally, the students are on the brink of a research project for which they have chosen a topic and are ready to begin initial stages of information seeking.

COOKING METHOD

1. To model, put the word *run* on the board and conduct a brainstorm session about terms associated with the word. As the group brainstorms, prompt students beyond the most obvious associations.
2. Ask students to enter *run* as a query into the discovery tool, noting the number of results. Students will open several records, identify the subject terms describing the item, and read the item's abstract, if one is available.
3. Next, explain how a discovery tool refines results based on the user's choices, and have students refine the results by subject, noticing the list of subject terms associated with their initial query. In pairs, students discuss different directions the query led to, and compare their results to the initial brainstorm on the board.
4. In pairs, students predict subject terms related to a new word, for example, *culture*. After writing these down, students

run this search in the discovery tool, refine by subject term, and compare the results to their brainstorm.

5. Students next complete a *Vocabulary Map* worksheet (Figure 1). The worksheet begins with a term, like *run* or *culture*, for example. Ideally, this term should have multiple meanings to allow for diverse subject term results. The worksheet guides students to see the interconnections between vocabulary by using a tree hierarchy to match the process of searching and refining by subject terms related to a word. After running the search, students record two related subject terms, limit the search results to each of these words, and record the number of results. This step is repeated for each of the new subject terms, leaving the student with four subject terms. For each of these four terms, the students choose and record a relevant resource from the refined result list.

6. After completing the worksheet, students use their own research topic and brainstorm keywords to use in their search. They predict subject terms associated with those keywords, and run a search in the discovery tool to confirm. While this occurs, encourage students to add terms to their list based upon the results.

7. Give students the abstracts from academic articles that you gathered prior to the lesson. They work in pairs to guess what subject terms would correspond with the abstracts. Provide students with answers after a short discussion.

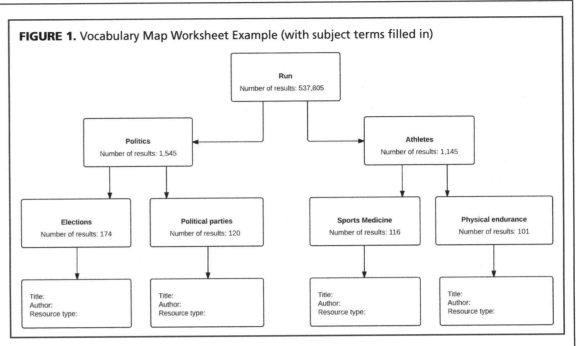

FIGURE 1. Vocabulary Map Worksheet Example (with subject terms filled in)

8. Give students a set of subject terms from which to write a brief abstract of their own. Discuss the relationship between the subject terms and the finished abstract.

ALLERGY WARNINGS

Depending on the level of language proficiency and academic familiarity of your students, library jargon and academic formats may be unfamiliar and confusing. Make sure to spend time thoroughly explaining items such as abstracts, databases, and subject terms. Providing students with a glossary of these concepts may be helpful. If learners' reading level is too low for abstracts, a discussion/practice on reading strategies (skimming, scanning and detailed comprehension) may be helpful before this lesson or within in, before Step 7.

CHEF'S NOTE

In choosing initial search examples, make sure to choose queries that can lead to several different groups of subject terms due to the queries' multiple meanings. This will allow for greater practice of word associations for ELLs.

CLEAN UP

At the end of the lesson, assess students' comprehension by their ability to:

- Demonstrate the ability to make word associations and use subject terms by using the *Vocabulary Map* effectively to document their searches (Step 5).

- Use their new skills to search successfully for their own topic (Step 6). Worksheets could be collected at Step 6 and reviewed to check for misunderstanding or confusion.
- Brainstorm possible subject terms for the provided abstracts (Step 7). Here, it would be unrealistic to expect students to guess the actual subject terms; however, they may come up with interesting or even more descriptive ones with encouragement. The goal is to have them think about the key ideas in the text and the associated subject terms that might capture these key ideas in a search.
- Write an abstract that addresses the given subject terms and meets the teacher's criteria for successful writing (Step 8).

Wholesale Distribution

Amy F. Fyn, Coordinator of Library Instruction, Coastal Carolina University, afyn@coastal.edu

NUTRITION INFORMATION

Faculty recommendations greatly influence student use of specific library resources. This lesson plan introduces faculty members to the discovery tool in a professional development session in order to promote use of this research tool.

Learning Outcomes

Students (faculty) will be able to:

- Articulate discovery tool contents in order to advocate for its use in relevant assignments.
- Use discovery tool limiters in order to retrieve a more relevant set of search results.
- Use advanced features of the discovery tool in order to save and organize information.

NUMBER SERVED

2 to 10 faculty

COOKING TIME

Prep time: Up to 30 minutes
Lesson delivery: 60 minutes

DIETARY GUIDELINES

Frame: Searching as Strategic Exploration

Knowledge Practices:

- Match information needs and search strategies to appropriate search tools.
- Design and refine needs and search strategies as necessary, based on search results.

Dispositions:

- Understand that first attempts at searching do not always produce adequate results.
- Realize that information sources vary greatly in content and format and have varying relevance and value, depending on the needs and nature of the search.

INGREDIENTS & EQUIPMENT

- Instructor station
- Projector
- Student computers

PREPARATION

- Design a presentation that includes at least five slides:
  - » What the discovery tool encompasses
  - » What is not found in the discovery tool
  - » When not to use the discovery tool (scenarios)
  - » When it's best to use the discovery tool
  - » Discovery tool search tips
- Market the session to faculty and/or graduate teaching assistants well in advance.

- Before the session, review the registration sign up and briefly research dissertations/research interests of faculty attendees. Alternately, faculty can be asked to indicate their research interests when signing up for the session.

COOKING METHOD

Starter

1. Invite faculty to share why they signed up for the session and what they hope to learn. Ask about their impression of and/or experience with the discovery tool. Acknowledge praise and concerns, and assure them that you will address both in the session.

2. Briefly introduce the discovery tool, including where to locate it on the library website, explain how it works and where it harvests or draws data from (presentation slides may help keep this section organized).

   a. What library content can be found in it and what cannot? What percent of database and journal content is searched through the discovery tool? Speak directly to some of the most relevant discipline-specific tools used by the faculty in attendance, along with at least one solid multi-disciplinary powerhouse.

3. Mention the specific strengths of the tool, such as its interdisciplinary nature. It's a simple way to search across many of the library's resources, and students like searching from one search box. Give at least two examples of research scenarios in which you'd use the tool.

4. Acknowledge weaknesses of the discovery tool or when it might be better to use a different resource. Discuss how these tools lack a unifying formal thesaurus and controlled vocabulary, and how they might not integrate consortial materials.

Mangia!

5. Hands-on time.
   a. Search for known items (book, article title [tip: it's even better when searching for titles whose author is in the room]).
   b. Request an exploratory search topic from the attendees and view the results, modeling adjusting as needed (faculty need reminders of good search practices too).
   c. Point out limiters, refinement options, and any bells and whistles the discovery tool has that improves the research experience. Challenge them to e-mail a set of results with a generated citation to themselves.

6. Ask volunteers to do a side-by-side comparison of discovery results vs. the results in their preferred discipline tool and/or Google Scholar. What differences do they spot? How does this tool affect or enhance their own research? How might it affect their students research?

Dessert

7. Challenge faculty to consider how their students can use the discovery tool in their assignments. Open the discussion if time permits.

ALLERGY WARNINGS
Advertise the workshop in advance and require signups so you can tailor the session to the attendees' research interests. Emphasize to faculty that the discovery service is not replacing their favorite databases. Be prepared to have an increase in instruction requests and research appointments!

CHEF'S NOTE
Focus on the positives of the discovery tool. Make sure to address the faculty concerns about the tool.

CLEAN UP
Assessment questions used at the end of the session include:
- Did this session match the session description and learning outcomes?
- What did you like about using the discovery tool?
- What did you dislike about using the discovery tool?
- What changes do you expect to make to assignments and/or how you conduct research as a result of this session?

- Would you like the librarian to follow up with you after the session? If yes, please give your contact information here.

Is Greed Good?
Using Research to Make Informed, Evidence-Based Decisions

Jeff Miller, Social Studies Educator, Sweet Home Middle School, jmiller@sweethomeschools.org; Melissa Langridge, Coordinator of User Education, Niagara University, mlangridge@niagara.edu; Bridget Doloresco, Outreach Librarian, Niagara University, bdoloresco@niagara.edu

NUTRITION INFORMATION

This lesson will introduce high school students to college level research. Students will answer the Inquiry Question: "Is Greed Good?" The students' active engagement in this unit will help them better understand the abuses of power by some capitalists and political leaders and the importance of civic responsibility to guard against such abuses in the future.

Students will use the library discovery tool to locate facts to support their research to complete the unit group project worksheet. Students will work with their groups to complete the questions in *Step 2: Production, Step 3: Advertisement,* and *Step 4: Selling Stock.* Students should already know how to locate, evaluate, and cite sources to successfully complete this activity.

Learning Outcomes
Students will be able to:
- Search a discovery tool using various keyword strategies in order to retrieve appropriate sources.
- Develop topic-relevant vocabulary in order to search the discovery tool with maximum flexibility and effectiveness.

NUMBER SERVED

Minimum of four; up to the maximum capacity of computers in library

COOKING TIME

Prep time: two hours
Cooking time: 40 to 80 minutes (dependent upon block scheduling availability)

DIETARY GUIDELINES

Frame 1: Research as Inquiry

Knowledge Practice:
Synthesize ideas gathered from multiple sources.

Disposition:
Appreciate that a question may appear to be simple but still disruptive and important to research; seek multiple perspectives during information gathering and assessment.

Frame 2: Information Creation as a Process

Knowledge Practice:
Develop, in their own creation processes, an understanding that their choices impact the purposes for which the information product will be used and the message it conveys.

Dispositions:
- Value the process of matching an information need with an appropriate product.
- Understand that different methods of information dissemination with different purposes are available for their use.

INGREDIENTS & EQUIPMENT
- Computer Lab
- "Industrialization and Immigration Performance Task: Is Greed Good?" worksheet
- Kahoot! quiz game (see Chef's Notes)

PREPARATION
- This lesson is part of a unit on industrialization and immigration and uses a flipped classroom approach. Students need to complete *Step 1: Create Your Company—Pick an Invention* on their worksheet prior to library instruction.

COOKING METHOD
1. Have students take out their worksheets (Figure 1).
2. Students will break up into groups of four. Each student will be assigned one of the following questions from their worksheet

FIGURE 1. Industrialization and Immigration Performance Task

INQUIRY QUESTION: "IS GREED GOOD?"
In this unit you will be given a character. Your mission is to successfully move your character from Europe to America and start a successful life in the New World. You and your teammates must accomplish the following:

Create a Business and Market an Invention
America is the "land of opportunity". You can make your fortune by starting a new business, manufacturing, and selling a product. Use the library discovery tool to locate sources that support your research to complete the unit group project worksheet. Work with your group to complete the questions in *Step 2: Production, Step 3: Advertisement, and Step 4: Selling Stock.* You will locate, evaluate, and cite sources to successfully complete this activity.

INDUSTRIALIZATION
Step 1: Create Your Company—Pick an Invention
Think about which products would be most useful to 19th Century businesses. Explain what your product is and which industry (railroads, steel, oil) would be helped the most by your product. Work with your group to pick a product to manufacture and sell.

Step 2: Production
Once you have created an idea for a product, you will need workers to produce it. As an employer you need to do the following:
A. *Will you hire union workers or non-union workers to build their product?*
B. *Will you pay extra to keep your factory safe for your workers or will you try to keep your costs as low as possible to maximize profit?*
C. *Will you choose to pay for high-quality materials or average quality materials?*
D. *Will you choose to use a quick means of transportation (railroads) or a slow means of transportation (wagon or canal) to bring raw materials (trees, oil, iron) to the factory.*

Step 3: Advertisement
A. *Create an advertisement for your chosen product. Include the purpose and target audience for your chosen product.*

Step 4: Selling Stock
In order to keep your company in business and have money to create your product you will have to
A. *Sell ownership of your company to the public via stocks. The better your product the more stock you will sell and the more money you will make.*

Each table will start with $1000. You must spend all of it to develop your product.

STEP 1: CREATE YOUR COMPANY—PICK AN INVENTION
Directions: As a group your table should agree on an invention and how it will be produced. Once that is done, each person in the group will have a task in the selling and buying of stock.

Name of Company: _____

Name of Product: _____

Description of the Product: _____

a. Student 1: Step 2: Production, Qs A & B
b. Student 2: Step 2: Production, Qs C & D
c. Student 3: Step 3: Advertisement, Q A
d. Student 4: Step 4: Selling Stock, Q A

3. Introduce students to the concept of historical research. What types of sources would you use to access historical information? What type of information would a historical newspaper provide? Why would it be useful in this assignment? Briefly describe how these sources, in addition to their textbook readings, should be used to further their understanding of concepts and application of knowledge.

4. Demonstrate sample search in the discovery tool to locate one historical news article and show types of information available in page view (advertisements, stories, etc.), including how to use the citation formatting option.

5. Play Kahoot!, a free game-based quiz, to evaluate students' knowledge on the types of sources they would use to answer each of the questions on their worksheet (Figure 2).

FIGURE 2. Kahoot!

FIGURE 1. Industrialization and Immigration Performance Task (continued)

STEP 2: PRODUCTION INFORMATION
Production Information:
Check one of each category. Remember you must spend $1000.00!

Labor

_____Union Workers (Cost—$500.00)   _____Non-Union Workers (Cost—$300.00)

Rationale: _____

Cite Evidence Used to Support Rationale:_____

Safety

_____ Above Safety Code Factory (Cost—$200.00)   _____ At Safety Code Factory (Cost—$100.00)

Rationale: _____

Cite Evidence Used to Support Rationale:_____

Materials

_____ Top of the Line Raw Materials (Cost- $300.00)   _____ Average Raw Materials (Cost—$100.00)

Rationale: _____

Cite Evidence Used to Support Rationale:_____

Total Money Spent Thus Far: $1000.00 – Labor – Safety – Materials = $ _____

Transportation

_____ Transportation Costs of Raw Materials to Factory _____ Transportation Costs of Goods to Factory
      (1 to 3 days transportation–Cost—$300.00)   (4–6 days transportation–Cost—$100.00)

Rationale: _____

Cite Evidence Used to Support Rationale:_____

Advertising

_____ National Advertising of Product (Cost—$400.00) _____ Local Advertising of Product (Cost—$200.00)

Rationale: _____

Cite Evidence Used to Support Rationale:_____

Total Money Spent Thus Far:
$ Money Remaining From Previous Page $ _____ – Transportation – Advertising = $ _____

6. Students will independently complete their worksheet questions as assigned. Upon completion of the questions, students will reconvene with their group to share their results.
7. Librarian will ask for a volunteer from each group to debrief the entire class on what their group found.

ALLERGY WARNINGS

A previous library instruction session will have introduced students to keyword searching, types of sources, and evaluation of sources. Be sure that your discovery tool indexes reference sources, historical newspapers, and the *Historical Statistics of the United States*. If your library does not own a print copy of this, an open source edition can be found via the U.S. Census website. Be sure to verify that the sources have been indexed before the class. You may also include the link in an accompanying course guide.

CHEF'S NOTE

The authors of this lesson have made the Kahoot! quiz game available for your use. To access it, sign up for a free Kahoot! account at Kahoot.it, then search the pool of quizzes for "Is Greed Good? Using Research to Make Informed, Evidence-Based Decisions."

CLEAN UP

Students will be assessed through observation and formative assessment. This guided practice gets students in the habit of citing sources and determining how carefully selected sources will be used.

Cold and Spicy Call Number Soup with Noodle Salad:
Serving Up a Banquet for International Students/English as a Second Language (ESL) Learners

Leila June Rod-Welch, Outreach Services Librarian, Assistant Professor, University of Northern Iowa, leila.rod-welch@uni.edu

NUTRITION INFORMATION

This recipe will introduce ESL leaners to basic library resources as many academic libraries in the United States are so different than academic libraries overseas. For example, some do not have open stacks and many ESL learners do not know how to read a call number as a result of this. ESL learners will be instructed on how to read a call number and how to conduct basic and advanced searches to find books using the discovery tool. Students will then receive three colored noodles (i.e., strips of paper) of two book titles and one author. The students will apply what they have learned by using the discovery tool to find these three books in the library.

Learning Outcomes
Students will be able to:
- Use the discovery tool to execute both basic and advanced search techniques.
- Read and understand a call number.
- Distinguish the location of the various collections in the library.

NUMBER SERVED

It will serve eight students. For larger groups, an assistant is recommend to help out with the activity. Students will get more assistance when the group is smaller.

COOKING TIME

Preparation time: 60 minutes the first time. Try to find uncommon author names to help students practice differentiating names of authors and book titles. Preparation time for future classes: Approximately 20 minutes. What takes the most time is making sure the books are available and not checked out.

50 minutes of library instruction to execute the lesson plan.

DIETARY GUIDELINES

Frame: Searching as Strategic Exploration

Knowledge Practices:
- Understand how information systems (i.e., collections of recorded information) are organized in order to access relevant information.
- Manage searching processes and results effectively.

Dispositions:
- Seek guidance from experts, such as librarians, researchers, and professionals.
- Persist in the face of search challenges, and know when they have enough information to complete the information task.

INGREDIENTS & EQUIPMENT

- Titles of eight books that are in the stacks and available for checkout.
- Titles of eight books that are in particular collections in the library and available for checkout.
- Authors of eight books that are in the stacks and available for checkout.
- A PowerPoint to introduce library terminology such as LC call number, decimal number, stacks, collection, availability, location, and check out to help ESL learners understand the meaning of these words.
- Find a YouTube video on how to read a call number or create your own.
- One computer or laptop for each student (or library instruction room equipped with multiple computers).

PREPARATION

This recipe requires a fair amount of advance preparation. It requires creating a PowerPoint to introduce library terminology. This PowerPoint can be used over and over for future classes. In addition, it requires searching for book titles that are available for checkout in the stacks. It also requires searching for book titles that are available for checkout in particular collections in the library. As well, we will need a list of authors with unique names (e.g. not John Smith). It is helpful if these authors only have one book in the library collection in order to reduce confusion and the number of students' questions about what book is the correct book. Each student receives three noodle strips. One noodle strip includes the title of a book in the stacks, one has the title of a book that is located in a particular collection of the library, and one has an author's name.

COOKING METHOD

1. Introduce the terminology by using PowerPoint (LC call number, decimal number, stacks, collection, availability, location, and check out) to help ESL learners understand the meaning of these words in the library context.

2. Watch a YouTube video about how to read a call number. This will reinforce the terminology by giving ESL learners a visual of the process to locate a book.

3. Demonstrate to the students how to conduct a basic search and an advanced search using the discovery tool.

4. Students will receive three colored noodles. They will first need to identify whether the name on the noodle strips are book titles or author names. Explain to students that for an author search, they will need to type the author's last name before the author's first name.

5. Demonstrate the discovery tool features that will help them in their task. Since the tool locates books, scholarly articles, newspaper articles, etc., all at once

unless otherwise specified, students will need to remember to check the box that searches for books only. Next, students need to change the "keyword search" to either a "title search" or an "author search," depending on their noodle strips.

6. In some cases, students may get several search results. For example, the library might have both a printed and an electronic version of the same book. Students need to identify which book is the print version as this is the book they need to bring back to class.

7. When students locate the entry for their noodle strips, they need to write down the location and call number of their noodle strip items. Students are instructed to bring these books back to the classroom. The first three students who bring back the correct books will receive a small prize.

ALLERGY WARNINGS

Time sensitivity: Make sure that the students check with the librarian before leaving class to look for their items. This allows them to confirm whether they have the correct call numbers. This saves time in the long run as sometimes students do not pay careful attention to the location of the materials. Once students have the correct information, they are allowed to leave the classroom to find the actual books. Students may get lost in the library, as well. If possible, it is helpful to have an assistant help out at this time so that students do not get lost in the

stacks. It can be too much excitement for some students, especially for those who are competitive.

CHEF'S NOTES

Some spices (prizes) such as stress balls, pens, other library promotional materials, or candy will add to the flavor of this dish. For example, I often reward the first three students back to the classroom with the correct books. Also, the instructor of the ESL class can reward students who completed the assignment correctly by awarding extra points to them. As well, I hand out prizes to students who answer questions correctly or if they make a good point throughout the class.

CLEAN UP

There is a follow-up assignment created by the ESL instructor that their students need to complete after the library visit. Students who fail the assignment must meet with an assigned librarian to review this session.

Which Came First:
The Whale or the Egg?

Dr. A. M. Salaz, Reference & Instruction Librarian, Carnegie Mellon University in Qatar, asalaz@cmu.edu; Teresa MacGregor, Director of the Library, Carnegie Mellon University in Qatar, teresam@qatar.cmu.edu

NUTRITION INFORMATION

For a short information literacy session that introduces the strengths and limitations of discovery tools, present students with a written question that contains ambiguity and lacks context. Then ask them to find the answers by searching library systems without the aid of additional human interaction. Wrap up the experience—designed to draw out common frustrations—with a review of best practices when first investigating an information need. This lesson is particularly useful for helping both ESL and non-ESL students examine the role of language and vocabulary in describing information needs and in expanding and narrowing search.

Learning Outcomes

Students will be able to:

- Analyze the clues within a stated information need in order to determine the best sources to meet that need.
- Apply basic and advanced search techniques to refine their results both on the web and within library discovery tools.
- Identify and critique the operational strengths and limitations of library discovery systems through experimentation and comparison with web searching.

NUMBER SERVED

5 to 15 students

COOKING TIME

Preparation time: 30 to 45 minutes (less if you are re-using questions/clues)
Lesson delivery: 1 hour. (This could be split into two sessions or "flipped" with the student exercise occurring at one time, for 15 to 30 minutes, and the explanation occurring afterward, for 30 minutes).

DIETARY GUIDELINES

Frame: Searching as Strategic Exploration

Knowledge Practices:
- Utilize divergent (e.g., brainstorming) and convergent (e.g., selecting the best source) thinking when searching.
- Understand how information systems (i.e., collections of recorded information) are organized to access relevant information.

Dispositions:
- Understand that first attempts at searching do not always produce adequate results.
- Persist in the face of search challenges, and know when enough information completes the information task.

INGREDIENTS & EQUIPMENT

- Internet-enabled computer (in the library or a lab)
- One copy of original question and one copy of (visual) clue per student
- One copy (minimum) of print or e-book containing the answer (e.g. *Dream Cars*). Substitutions encouraged!
- Classroom time for follow-up presentation (script provided, Figure 2) and Q&A
- Instructor station and projector (for follow-up presentation)

PREPARATION

- Instruct on-duty library staff about how much or how little help they are expected to provide to students during the exercise.
- If available in print, stage the target book (e.g. *Dream Cars*) in the desired location.
- Print copies of the handouts (question and visual clue) for each student.

COOKING METHOD

1. Gather students in the library and present them with the following questions: Which came first: the whale or the egg?
   a. What are the whale and the egg (provide a general description)?
   b. Name a person associated with the whale and the egg?

c. When were the whale and the egg invented?

d. Can you find a print source in the library that includes information on the whale and the egg? Provide the source name, location in the library, and location of the information within the source.

2. After 5 to 10 minutes of struggling, provide students with a second, visual clue:

3. Give students another 5 to 10 minutes to discover the answer (Figure 1).

4. Follow up immediately after the exercise with a discussion on the challenges encountered, the behavior of the search systems utilized, and the best approaches to interacting with systems in ways that are likely to produce the desired results.

"The Egg." Early electric car prototype, as shown on page 66 in Schleuning, S. & Gross, K. (2014). *Dream cars: Innovative design, visionary ideas*. Atlanta, Georgia: High Museum of Art.

The image above is a placeholder only. Due to copyright constraints, we cannot print the actual image here. However, under fair use rules, you could use the actual image from the text in your teaching materials.

FIGURE 1. Spoiler Alert—Answer Key

Which came first: the whale or the egg?

The Whale (*La Baleine*) predated the Egg (*L'Œuf*) by four years

- What are the whale and the egg (provide a general description)?
  Early electric car designs or vintage electric concept cars
  The Whale = *La Baleine*
  The Egg = *L'Œuf*

- Name a person associated with the whale and the egg?
  Paul Arzens, French artist, sculptor, and designer

- When were the whale and the egg invented?
  The Whale (*La Baleine*) = 1938
  The Egg (*L'Œuf*) = 1942

Can you find a print source in the library that includes information on the whale and the egg? Provide the source name, location in the library, and location of the information within the source.

> *Dream Cars: Innovative Design, Visionary Ideas*
> Book
> Call Number: TL7 .U62A85 2014
> Library catalog entry: http://search.library.cmu.edu/vufind/Record/1575744
> Location: Q-Display (Qatar Display Area)
> Pages 66–69
>
> **{ Will vary by library, of course }**

---

5. Incorporate a presentation on analyzing information needs and, in particular, how to use library discovery tools to answer those needs (Figure 2). This question-driven presentation may focus on issues generated through the activity, such as:

a. Disambiguation of concepts through the use of specific language and keywords.

b. Functionality within discovery tools such as "Related Terms," inclusions, and exclusions.

c. The links between electronic records and physical items such as locators, call numbers, and other metadata.

d. The challenges of description and classification.

ALLERGY WARNINGS

Having only one copy of the target resource when the exercise must accommodate many students may create a bottleneck. Consider resource-to-student ratios when designing the activity.

This activity is run once per academic year. Questions, clues, and solutions are changed every year to prevent answers being leaked among students.

CHEF'S NOTES

We have used this lesson plan several times with undergraduates in information systems courses, such as mobile application development and human-computer interaction. It works especially well with students in these disciplines.

Use of this exercise in a transnational ESL environment creates special linguistic and cultural challenges and opportunities related to resource description, keyword searching, and interactions with systems.

We recommend capitalizing on this with a liberal sprinkling of discussion on how discovery tools match (or fail to match) text and synonyms in descriptive records. Add more flavor with a discussion of bias (cultural, gender, academic, etc.). Do the discovery tools themselves carry bias? How can researchers understand and counter such biases?

This particular activity works only if you have the appropriate source in your library. In this case, the book titled *Dream Cars* (Schleuning, S. & Gross, K. (2014). *Dream cars: Innovative design, visionary ideas*. Atlanta, Georgia: High Museum of Art.). Substitutions are encouraged. We have used the same lesson design with other clues/books, such as "Show me the little tramp dining on unusual spaghetti" with the visual clue:

Charlie Chaplin as The Little Tramp eating shoelaces like spaghetti, from the movie *The Gold Rush* (1925), as shown on page 154 in Vance, J. (2003). *Chaplin: Genius of the cinema*. New York: Harry N. Abrams.

The image to the right is a placeholder only. Due to copyright constraints, we cannot print the actual image here. However, under fair use rules, you could use the actual image from the text in your teaching materials.

FIGURE 2. Library Research Challenge
Which Came First: The Whale or The Egg?
Best Practices for Research

When presented with an information need, the first thing to do is to get more information (a.k.a. background searching).

1. Ask questions
   a. Who or what is the whale? Who or what is the egg?
   b. If the whale and the egg were "invented" what could they be and/or not be?

2. Get more information
   a. Google it!
   b. *Wikipedia* it!
   [Run a Google search on: whale and egg. Show that the results do not help answer the provided questions.]

3. Get even more information
   a. Use smart search features such as putting full phrases in quotation marks
   [Run a Google search on: "the whale" and "the egg." Show that the results are getting closer, but still are not enough to answer the provided questions.]

4. Get still more information
   a. Seek out other clues such as keywords, synonyms, and images
   [Run a Google search on: "the whale" and "the egg" car. Show that the results are on point. Switch to Google Images to see the same image as provided in the clue (Student Handout 2). Cracked it!]

5. Follow the trail
   a. Now take your new information and find resources in the library
   [Run searches in the library's discovery tool. Show varying results with different keywords (l'oeuf, "the egg," arzens, concept car) and collections. Ultimately, navigate to the correct title in the catalog.]

6. Lessons Learned
   a. To find information, you need more information. Computers are dumb. They don't know anything about context
   b. Ask questions. A librarian will interview you at the Reference Desk. Sometimes you have to interview yourself.
   c. Google it or Wikipedia it.
   d. Seek out other clues (keywords, synonyms, images).
   e. Follow the trail.
   f. Search on the library website.
   g. The right answer may be in more than one location.

7. Questions?

CLEAN UP

Assessment of this activity is conducted informally and formatively using open discussion and reflection on the search processes and analysis of the systems employed. Students' expressed observations and understandings of search system functionality, shortcomings, and strengths should aid and inform discussion of how to better interact with and manipulate these systems.

Assessment of this activity can be conducted formally by asking students to subsequently develop proposals for improving search system functionality, providing them with an opportunity to think critically about the utility of discovery systems for research and to show understanding of these systems' strengths and limitations.

ADDITIONAL RESOURCES

- Print or e-book (e.g., Schleuning, S. & Gross, K. (2014). *Dream cars: Innovative design, visionary ideas*. Atlanta, Georgia: High Museum of Art.)
- Research question and (visual) clue handouts
- Answer Key
- Follow-up presentation script

6. ROOM SERVICE
flipping the classroom

Discovery Layers and the Flipped Classroom:
Recipe for Success!

Cara Berg, Reference Librarian/Co-Coordinator of User Education, William Paterson University, bergc1@wpunj.edu

NUTRITION INFORMATION

Most students enrolled in FYS (First Year Seminar) at William Paterson University attend a one-shot library instruction class. We use a flipped classroom model where, prior to attending the class and on their own time, the students watch two brief videos and complete a cognitive exercise. One video is about plagiarism and the other is a tutorial on how to use the library's discover layer. During the class, the librarian then guides students through the discovery tool; letting students lead the class while the librarian helpfully provides them with hints throughout the demonstration. Students are assessed with an in-class assignment to find and cite an e-book, and by locating an article based on a keyword search. The flipped classroom allows the students to be more engaged in the class and allows for more time to cover other topics during the one-shot.

Learning Outcomes

Students will be able to:

- Recognize the importance of seeking assistance from a librarian and identify core library resources and services.
- Search discovery tool for library materials.
- Recognize when it's appropriate to use the discovery tool, and when it's appropriate to use other sources.

NUMBER SERVED

Approximately 20 students per class

COOKING TIME

75 minutes, including the time for the in-class assessment and a separate portion on website evaluation. The discovery tool portion of the instruction takes about 40 minutes.

DIETARY GUIDELINES

Frame 1: Information has Value

Knowledge Practice:
Give credit to the original ideas of others through proper attribution and citation.

Disposition:
Respect the original ideas of others.

Frame 2: Searching as Strategic Exploration

Knowledge Practices:
- Design and refine needs and search strategies as necessary, based on search results.
- Manage searching processes and results effectively.

Dispositions:
- Realize that information sources vary greatly in content and format and have varying relevance and value, depending on the needs and nature of the search.
- Seek guidance from experts, such as librarians, researchers, and professionals.

INGREDIENTS & EQUIPMENT

- Video: How to Use the Discovery Layer
- Video: Plagiarism Tutorial
- Video: Library Tour (for in-class viewing)
- Google Forms (to create the assignment)
- Classroom management software (such as Lanschool) that allows you to push the assignment page to students while they are at their computers in class. A TinyURL with the link works just as well.
- Computer lab (optional)

PREPARATION

- Send the instructor the links to the videos so that he/she can assign students to watch the videos prior to coming to class.
- The students' professor receives automatically generated e-mails when students have completed the videos. Students are also asked to name one thing they learned after watching the videos.

- The librarian teaching the class can check the response page in Google Forms to see which students have watched the video and the students' response to what they learned.

COOKING METHOD

1. Before they come to class, the students view the two videos and complete a cognitive exercise.
2. Begin with a quick video tour of the library.
3. Demonstrate the discovery tool. Since the students have already viewed the videos, the demonstration is more of an active learning experience for the students. For example, instead of showing the students how to narrow down your results by date range, ask students what they would do.
4. Next, the students are given their assignment (Figure 1). They complete Part I, which asks them to locate an e-book in the discovery tool and copy the citation.
5. The librarian leads the class in an activity and discussion on keywords. An image is shown in the class and the students supply keywords to describe that image.
6. Students work on section II of the assignment. They are again given an image and asked to list keywords that could describe that image. They then enter their keywords into the discovery tool to locate a scholarly, peer-reviewed article that they think closely matches their keywords.

FIGURE 1. First-Year-Seminar Library Assessment

Section 1:
1. Using the discovery tool, find the book, *What the Best College Students Do*. Copy the citation using **MLA format**.
2. Look at the record for the book. What do you see that indicates that the book is an e-book, not a print book?
   a. Says "electronic resource"
   b. Says "internet resource"
   c. Has a picture of the cover
   d. Has the call number listed
3. Open the book. Copy or write the **first sentence** of the **second paragraph of Chapter 3**.

Section 2:
1. Look at the image below. Write **at least 3 keywords** that would be good for finding more information about this image.

Image courtesy, US Government. "White House Logo". Digital Image. 2003. Wikiimedia Commons. https://commons.wikimedia.org/

2. Using your keywords from the previous question, do a search in the discovery tool. Find an **article** from an **academic journal** that you feel matches your search. Copy and paste the citation in **MLA format**.

7. After completing section II, students are asked if there are any remaining questions about using the discovery layer in the library.

ALLERGY WARNINGS

The class is very participation-heavy. Refrain from lecturing on the content in the videos the students watched prior to class as they will lose interest.

CHEF'S NOTE

Good communication with their instructor is key! The students were most likely to watch the videos prior to the class when instructors remind them of it.

CLEAN UP

Students were assessed in-class. They were also e-mailed a brief post-test at the end of the semester to check on their retention of the information. The post-test was optional, open for seven days, and e-mailed to them directly by the co-coordinator of the user education program in the library.

Poutine à la Carte:
Teaching Humanities Research to Graduate Students with a Discovery Tool

Éthel Gamache, Reference & Subject Librarian, Concordia University Libraries (Montréal, Québec, Canada), ethel.gamache@ concordia.ca

NUTRITION INFORMATION
This workshop is designed for humanities graduate students. Students from other disciplines are also welcome, as multidisciplinary research is encouraged. The aim of the workshop is to provide tools for graduate students to successfully answer their information needs toward the completion of their thesis. The lesson plan consists of various modules that can be mixed and matched based on time and class needs. It is a flipped classroom as students will evaluate and communicate their information needs prior to the workshop. At the end of this workshop, all attendees should be informed of key library services and be able to use general and key resources in the humanities.

Learning Outcomes
Students will be able to:
- Search using a discovery tool in order to retrieve background information, books and articles.
- Perform humanities-specific research in order to successfully inform their thesis.
- Recognize the research process in order to build a strong thesis, and eventually disseminate it.

NUMBER SERVED
15 to 25 participants

COOKING TIME
Prep time: 3 hours (Creating a survey, analyzing its data, and refocusing the teaching material.)
Lesson delivery: 75 to 90 minutes

DIETARY GUIDELINES
Frame 1: Scholarship as Conversation,

Knowledge Practices:
- Identify the contribution that particular articles, books, and other scholarly pieces make to disciplinary knowledge.
- Summarize the changes in scholarly perspective over time on a particular topic within a specific discipline.

Dispositions:
- See themselves as contributors to scholarship rather than only consumers of it
- Suspend judgment on the value of a particular piece of scholarship until the larger context for the scholarly conversation is better understood

Frame 2: Searching as Strategic Exploration

Knowledge Practices:
- Match information needs and search strategies to appropriate search tools.
- Understand how information systems (i.e., collections of recorded information) are organized in order to access relevant information.

Dispositions:
- Exhibit mental flexibility and creativity.
- Persist in the face of search challenges, and know when they have enough information to complete the information task.

INGREDIENTS & EQUIPMENT
- Survey creation tool
- Library website and discovery layer
- Flexibility

PREPARATION
- At least a week before the workshop, prepare a survey addressed to students in which they will assess their ability and comfort in searching different elements. Include questions about their research projects (if they have a topic, a specific research question, and identified main keywords) and a space for them to share any comments.

- Identify what you wish to transmit to graduate humanities students and create learning modules—ad hoc lessons—on each topic you want to explore with them. Aim for 3 to 4 modules at a time in order not to get overwhelmed. Prepare the learning modules in advance.
  Possible topics:
  - » Research and its process
  - » Getting started: background information
  - » Finding books and articles
  - » Finding popular media, video and audio
  - » Finding primary sources and historical newspapers
  - » Finding humanities specific resources
  - » Using a bibliographic management tool with a discovery layer
  - » Using Google Scholar
- The lesson may be tailored to their interest, either by weight given to each part or by skipping a module all together, depending of the homogeneity of the group. This is useful as students come with different backgrounds and different abilities.

COOKING METHOD

1. As with any poutine, there are three key ingredients:
   a. introducing yourself and the aim of the workshop (the fries)
   b. informing the students of the key library services and resources, especially those offered exclusively to graduate students (the curds)
   c. highlighting the importance of keeping track of research and resources used in order to avoid plagiarism (the gravy)
2. Review the survey results with the group. Clarifications or new questions might arise.
3. Based on class discussion about the survey responses, some steps from your ad-hoc lesson may be modified. The instructor must be very careful to keep a logical flow between the modules. We suggest to give more weight to modules that have gathered more interest, while lightly reviewing modules that are well understood.
4. Pick and choose from the modules below depending on time and class needs (points 5 to 11).
5. Module 1: Discuss research, scholarship and the research process itself with the students. We use the ACRL *Scholarship as Conversation* or *Searching as Strategic Exploration* to spark the discussion. It is interesting to see how, as graduate students are kick starting their academic careers, they have experimented with research and how they see themselves as part of the process. When we talk about *Scholarship as Conversation,* I ask them if they see themselves as researchers, the impact they wish to have and if they consider to be part of a scholar community. I use *Searching as Strategic Exploration* to accent how research is iterative, and to encourage them in persevering. I talk about my own experience during my master thesis, and prompt them to share their experiences with their own research projects.
6. Module 2: Getting started
   a. Explain the use of an encyclopedia in getting all the key information on a specific subject.
   b. Discuss how to create a research equation with keywords, synonyms and Boolean operators. Give examples of how limiters are useful.
   c. Show how to use the discovery tool to find online and print encyclopedias. Use keywords from a research question submitted in the survey.
   d. Have the students do this exercise with their own research question.
7. Module 3: Explain how to search for books and articles in the discovery tool. If available, use a research question identified in the survey.
   a. Identify keywords with the group and use them in the discovery tool. (You can either use the same keywords as used in 6b) for continuity, or identify new keywords from another research topic shared in the survey.) Launch search. Use facets and limiters to narrow the search.
   b. Show the catalogue record of a pertinent document. Make sure all new students are familiar with the location (which library, which floor) or in-house vocabulary used in the catalogue (e.g. tags, on the shelf/

available). Take this opportunity to show additional actions, such as save, e-mail, cite, tag.

c. Make sure to review the differences between magazines and peer-reviewed or scholarly journals and show how to differentiate them. You can tie this with Module 1.

d. You may need to use other databases for historical newspapers and primary sources. Again, with a topic suggested in the survey, explore primary sources and how to identify them. Point to other resources in the libraries, such as archive services and specialized databases, to complete this module.

e. Give the students some minutes to try this with their own research question. At this point, we just aim for them to feel comfortable with the discovery tool.

8. Module 4: Show how to find popular media, video and audio in the discovery tool by using facets to narrow their search to format. The instructor can use a research question used in the modules above. This is a great opportunity to show the diversity of material in the collection (e.g. tapes, VHS, CD, streaming, vinyl), where to access them and where to use them.

9. Module 5:
a. Identify what the discovery tool can offer in humanities specific resources and its limits.

b. Show how other resources can also be useful. For example, finding scriptures will require a specific database.

c. If the students mentioned anything humanities specific in the survey or at the beginning of the workshop, new is an excellent time to answer these needs.

10. Module 6: Introduce the group to various bibliographic management tools. We prioritize the one promoted by the libraries, but it can be fruitful to also show a free tool. If your discovery tool allows exportation, show it.

11. Module 7: Discuss Google Scholar. This can include how to set up preferences in the settings or a discussion about information that can be found there.

12. Close the workshop by thanking students for their participation, creating a space for questions and suggesting they meet with their subject librarian for support in their thesis research.

ALLERGY WARNINGS

Remember some students may come from different disciplines and may not be familiar with the research process used in humanities Still, graduate students should have a strong academic background and can catch up pretty quickly. It is important to have a strong narrative, even if the modules could be taught independently, to keep the students engaged.

CHEF'S NOTES

This is a great way to cover many potential interests and to keep it interesting for the students. They partly self-asses in the survey, so their interest and curiosity are sparked. A handout with the key information tied to each module is given to all attending students. It can offer reminders of websites, key databases, specific procedures and your contact information. The handout can then take the form of a worksheet, where both information and exercises cohabit and reinforce each other.

CLEAN UP

At the end of the workshop, you can ask the students on a slip of paper what they learned today, what they are still confused about, and how the class could be improved. They can leave you their e-mail address if they would like a follow-up. Season to taste with your personality and creativity.

Pricing the Ingredients

Tammy Ivins, Transfer Student Services Librarian, University of North Carolina at Wilmington, ivinst@uncw.edu

NUTRITION INFORMATION

This flipped-classroom assignment is designed for use in a face-to-face, semester-long library course. (If the course is online or if you wish to use this activity as part of a one-shot library session, see the Allergy Warnings for substitutions). Student chefs will work in small groups to determine the monetary value of library resources. After this meal, student will understand issues around the access to information and the relative value of different information sources.

Learning Outcomes

Students will be able to:

- Articulate the monetary value of library resources and relative costs of different information sources.
- Understand financial disparity issues related to access to information.

NUMBER SERVED

5 to 50, in small groups.

COOKING TIME

Prep time: Allow 10 to 15 minutes of previous face-to-face class time to prep the student chefs on their flipped-classroom assignment. (If you are using this activity as part of a one-shot library session and will not meet the students prior to the session, see the Allergy Warnings for substitutions). Allow a week for students to complete 'cooking' up their research.

Cooking time: Class time is dependent on the number of groups, as each will be expected to present their findings. For five student groups, plan for a 50-minute class.

DIETARY GUIDELINES

Frame: Information has Value

Knowledge Practice:
Recognize issues of access or lack of access to information sources.

Dispositions:
- Value the skills, time, and effort needed to produce knowledge
- Are inclined to examine their own information privilege.

INGREDIENTS & EQUIPMENT

- A whiteboard/chalkboard or computer & project/large screen (see the Allergy Warnings for online classes).

PREPARATION

- Choose search topics, preferably from a wide range of disciplines. For example: Stem Cells, Pearl Harbor, Mars, and Shakespeare.
- At least one week prior to the class, the Head Chef (instructor) should explain the flipped classroom activity,

assign small groups & topics, demonstrate the activity, and answer any questions. (If you are using this activity as part of a one-shot library session and will not meet the students prior to the session, see the Allergy Warnings for substitutions).

COOKING METHOD

1. Prior to the class, the student chefs will work in groups to search your library's discovery tool using the topic that the librarian has assigned (Figure 1).
2. Students will take the first page of results (or, however many of the results you assign) and calculate how much it would cost to buy those results out-of-pocket.
   - » Books & Media: Students should use retail tools such as Google Books and Amazon.com to identify the retail value of every book result.
   - » Articles: Students should use the periodical's website to determine the cost of a yearly individual subscription for each journal result.
3. Students record both the total and average cost of the journal subscriptions, books, and media. They should prepare to serve or present their findings in class.
4. On the day of the class, the student groups should serve or present their searches and results to the class. 5 to 7 minutes each.

FIGURE 1. Assigned Topic Worksheet

Assigned topic: _____

Teammates: _____

Due date/ Presentation date: _____

Assignment purpose: You are going to calculate how much it would cost you to do research if you weren't a [insert your school here] student.

Divide-up the workload among your teammates and work together, but every member of the group must help.

1. **Search the Library's main search box for the topic** (above) your group has been assigned. You are going to look carefully at the results.

2. **Looking at the first page of results**, note the titles of every book and piece of media (DVDs, VHS CDs, etc.). Also note the periodical title (magazine, newspaper, journal, etc.) that each article result was published in.

3. **Calculate how much it would cost you to buy these items** out-of-pocket, if you weren't a student here.
   » Use retail tools such as Google Books and Amazon.com to identify the retail value of every book & piece of media.
   » For the periodicals, use the publishers' websites to determine the cost of a yearly individual subscription.

4. **Study the results and prepare** to present them to the class. At the very least, you must know:
   » The total out-of-pocket cost for all of the research materials
   » The average cost of a single periodical subscription, book, and piece of media.

5. In class, **present your findings** in 5 to 7 minutes. Your presentation must include:
   » Your topic
   » The total out-of-pocket cost for all of the research materials
   » The average cost of a single periodical subscription, book, and piece of media.
   » Any challenges & issues that you faced.
   » Your thoughts on your findings. Were you surprised?

Be prepared to answer any questions from your classmates.

5. While the students are presenting their searches and results to the class, the librarian should record the results in a way that all the students can see, either on a classroom whiteboard or a word processing document on a computer and projector screen. (If the course is online, see the Allergy Warnings for substitutions).

6. Finally, the class should "dine on" or discuss the results. Facilitate the discussion by referring students to the visible list of results and with questions such as:
   » What searches resulted in the most expensive results? Why?
   » What items cost the most? How about the least? Why?
   » Why do we pay for information?
   » Does the library pay the exact same amount that you just calculated?
   » How do you think these costs affect people trying to do independent research?

ALLERGY WARNING

You can use this recipe in an asynchronous online course. For Serving (the in-class presentation), have student chefs share their results using a wiki (or similar tool). For the Dining (in-class discussion), use a discussion board (or similar tool).

If you are using this activity as part of a one-shot library session and will not meet the students prior to the session, have the course instructor divide the students into groups and assign the activity. You may need to meet with the course instructor to explain the activity.

CLEAN UP

To reinforce the learning outcomes, remind students of this activity at other times during the semester (or, remind the course instructor to do so). Challenge students to think about how they would do research (or if they could) without their campus access.